The
New
Jews

The New Jews

Edited by JAMES A. SLEEPER
and ALAN L. MINTZ

VINTAGE BOOKS

A Division of Random House

New York

Acknowledgments

We are very glad to acknowledge the cooperation of the American Jewish Committee in the preparation of this book for publication, the more so because the Committee's intent has been to help in bringing these viewpoints and feelings to a broad readership without prescribing or limiting their content. To Yehuda Rosenman and Sonya Kaufer of the Committee go our special thanks for their reading of the manuscript and their helpful comments; their support has been characteristic of the Committee's willingness to facilitate the undertakings of young Jews in many fields without unduly shaping the initiative and direction. We are also grateful to Jane Seitz, Hilary Maddux, and Linda Darman of Random House for their editorial assistance and guidance. Of course the content remains our own, and while these individuals and their organizations fully deserve to share credit for the completion of this enterprise, they are not in any way responsible for the views of the authors.

Contents

Part Two

Religious Imagination

The
New
Jews

No one needs the saving connection with a people so much as the youth who is seized by spiritual seeking, carried off into the upper atmosphere by the intellect; but among the youths of this kind and this destiny, none so much as the Jewish. The other peoples preserve from dissolution the deep inborn binding to the native soil and popular tradition inherited from millennia. The Jew, even with a feeling for nature acquired since yesterday and a cultivated understanding of, say, German popular art and customs, is directly threatened by such dissolution and abandoned to it so far as he does not find himself at home in his community. And the most sparkling wealth of intellectuality, the most luxuriant seeming productivity . . . cannot compensate the detached man for the holy insignia of humanity—rootedness, binding, wholeness.

—Martin Buber

Introduction

by JAMES A. SLEEPER

The story of the Jewish people has been told many times. Its telling is especially difficult in an age characterized alternately by glib sloganeering and verbal detachment—an age in which words are cheap, commitments wordy. The Jew's story has been anything but glib and detached; it has been a long and paradox-ridden journey, passionate and engaged, flecked with unspeakable ecstasy and pain. So perhaps one need not be apologetic about the fact that he can begin to sketch even a small part of that journey only with something like a deep sigh.

But then this is also an age in which we who would retell the Jewish story have *learned* how to sigh—not, admittedly, from the burdens of deprivation and oppression, but from the hollowness of an affluence and a freedom which surround us with glibness, detachment, and meaninglessness.

3

Accordingly, this book must be viewed not only as a part of Jewish history, but also as a reflection of the fact that for most of its contributors, the American Dream of affluence and freedom has come true; we are at least temporary winners in mankind's massive, continuing struggle to be free of knocks in the night, of searchlights and torture and fear, of hunger and physical insecurity. But that is not enough for us—an assertion which must surely seem ironic and presumptuous to those who have known the terrors of the past, and who have dedicated their lives to freeing us from them, only to see us "play" with social alienation and repression as if these were toys.

Material security is not enough for us because we have learned anew that the "enlightened" perspectives of the affluent can be paralyzing, that pearls around the neck do not remove stones from upon the heart, that a sense of personal wholeness, a capacity to give and receive love and intimations of meaning and dignity in daily life do not come from material security, not even from "healthy adjustment" to the society which purveys that security in exchange for a surrender of soul.

We are not playing. American youth's quest is no longer entirely the traditional adolescent grasp at a socially acceptable identity, or a search for an at-homeness with the customs and symbols of the going national culture. America's socially acceptable identities are no longer fulfilling; they feel pasted on, and they leave a growing personal dissatisfaction. At-homeness with culture is no substitute for a deeper, more permanent at-oneness with cosmos and with others. Why are we not happily defined by our jobs and our neighborhoods, our nationalities and our nominal affiliations? Why do we ask for something deeper? Perhaps we are not at home with these current roles and symbols because for us they enshrine no great hopes, engage no passions, inspire no works of joy or spirit. It has fallen to us to rediscover, however imperfectly, the prophetic insight that reason and plenty are no substitutes for myth and fantasy and faith, after all.

Surely it is on these intangible but important levels that American "culture" has broken down, and our search is no longer the same as that of the adolescent and the ill who are expected to re-embrace it. The search for a deeper affirmation of life begins within the self and in basic relationships and small communities. It struggles beneath the stale crust of official ideologies and syntheses and symbols, drawing instead upon the suppressed, underground well-springs of fantasy and awe which must water even the toughest and most sophisticated of undertakings. So it is, at root, an existential and a religious search, a raw renewal of the courage to be. As such, it is a search which drives us back into the history of our people.

For this is a book by young Americans some of whose strongest living roots plunge deep into the human past. Much of their personal richness and complexity has grown up around the ancient Hebrew spirit. What is new about their tilling of the ancient, fertile ground is the perspective from which they approach it. Tradition is encountered not simply from within, but warily, from without, and with the new urgency of an age which is shaking the very foundations of the human self-image. Many of the contributors to this volume have wallowed for a time in the angst and alienation of our century, a time in which "all their bones" have proclaimed the absurdity of life, not the Glory of God.

Yet these roots live. Twisted, tough, and gnarled, Jewishness blossoms hesitantly in a seemingly inhospitable arena. To experience this paradox is to begin to understand the paradox of Jewish survival, the capacity of our tradition to press itself upon new frontiers of human awareness. It is not a question of "relevance"; we are not seminarians attempting intellectually to "shed light upon the present" through scholarship. Jewish survival and meaningfulness depend upon more than exegesis.

How, then, do Jewish roots speak? How does this people's experience resonate so powerfully in men caught in the crosscurrents of human change and consciousness, men flirting with nihilism, grasping at an affirmation of life?

Perhaps it begins as a curiosity. Jewishness becomes intriguing when you try to make sense out of the fact that as a Jew on the current scene you are a slumlord to blacks, a civil rights worker to Southern whites, a well-heeled business school opportunist to hippies, a student radical to Wasp conservatives, an Old Testament witness to Vermont Yankees, an atheist to Midwestern crusaders, a capitalist to leftists, a communist to rednecks.

Jewishness surfaces a bit more when, reflecting upon these contradictions, you become dimly aware of having at your fingertips a reservoir of treasures you cannot wholly use—of being a member of a people rich in folklore and fantasy, fiery with social prophecy, warm in love of home and family, holy in piety and scholarship, yet seemingly bereft of theological and popular underpinnings by the experience of Auschwitz, which shattered our faith in divine guidance and destroyed vital organic Jewish communities.

Gradually Jewishness becomes stronger, making claims upon your search for meaning, when you realize that, much more than the rest of mankind, your people have known what it is to live as pariahs in the universe, with the shadow of total annihilation a constant reality. In such moments of awareness a lesson of Jewish survival is "hope against hope." Hope when it makes no sense. Hope when you have known the seamy, brutal underside of a Church that stirs the hearts of millions, or when you have begun to understand the claim of a Jew dying in the Warsaw ghetto that he would be the oppressed rather than the oppressor if the choice must be made.

Then there is the claim of the emotions; for perhaps

the personal experience of this Jewish paradox lies simply in the way a warm, liquid kaleidoscope of memories and treasures eddies and flows within, surfacing unexpectedly to the embarrassment of your reason, and to the havoc of carefully calculated loyalties. Then the pain of Jewishness is felt: you must wander with this kaleidoscope—the memory of a gentle grandmother who lit a Sabbath candle and died, or of a Hasidic melody which at times makes your favorite "hard rock" seem like cheap tin—through the American Jewish community, a spiritual Hiroshima which has been the setting for the transformation of the Hebrew spirit into an increasingly dispensable appendage of middle-class aesthetics and culture.

And as you travel through the broad, chaotic, enslaved hothouse of American youth, stumbling over the movements, the idioms, and the "sell-outs," you realize that you are learning through your experiences as an *American* what it is to see the world through *Jewish* eyes—eyes deep with the past, a bit too sad for constant merrymaking, too wise for boisterous idealism, eyes that shine with rage and hope, but that glisten with tears when confronted with innocence. Perhaps it is that as injustice and dehumanization drive you to the margins of the American society, you experience the pull of a uniquely Jewish spirituality whose ecstasy is short-lived, and which by its nature thrusts you back ablaze into the social center. You begin to study the prophets, for example, and a hot desert wind blowing from across the centuries parches material pleasure and mystic abandon alike, permitting you only the self-fulfillment that comes from the drive to build men who are joyous through righteousness. You realize that those who confuse righteousness with "straight-laced Puritan rectitude" are only confirming what would be in the nature of a Jewish critique of our society—that we have been robbed by cynicism of a viable notion of righteousness in both language and experience: we have no word for it which does not seem stuffy; we are too seldom inspired by memories or models of its practice. By what magic word can you denote a sixth sense for justice, strong as fantasy, suffused with warm concern for humans, applied to daily life with lust? Your Jewishness has asked you this question; the roots have begun to speak.

And you realize that to be a Jew is to feel the power of Judaism's thunderous onslaught on solipsism and paralyzing detachment. You learn that while in the university you are free enough to experiment with many life-styles and modes of being, you are sometimes *too* free to experience the satisfactions that come of fidelity and deep commitment. Yours is the pain of self-consciousness; with seeming agility you slip into skullcap and prayer shawl, pretending for perhaps a minute or an hour to be what men before you were able to be—and forced to be—for a lifetime.

And so you have begun to feel the intensity with which a growing young self becomes fused to a historic tradition. At the same time, you know of the way in which current conditions make this intersection of self and history increasingly difficult to pull off. Gripped in the dark age of liberal intellectual education, you know that you cannot wait for science to solve the riddle of subjectivity, or irreducible self; that in the meantime, nevertheless, all commitments are arbitrary, all absolutes are metaphors, all sources of self-definition are conditional.

Can there be a "Jewish" response to this seemingly incurable detachment? What can be answered to the implicit claim of modern life that intuition and passion are "inappropriate" responses to the academy and the corporation, that the only meaningful commitment is that to discovery and to the enlargement of human power? Perhaps we must suggest that scientific discovery itself yields no priorities for humanity, that reason which suppresses the irrational subsoil from which it grew can do us little good. We need ways to express spiritual impulses in daily life, lest without channels for positive expression they return as demons to destroy us in the forms of Führers and bombs. But to express them we cannot always withdraw from Secular City in search of a private sanctuary for spirit; when warmth and common reverence and a sense of peoplehood are driven from the public places they cannot long survive anywhere else, nor can they hide from the public monster which inevitably replaces a sense of community. Perhaps, then, it is a lesson of Jewish history that the collective consciousness of society can no more remain starved for faith and fantasy and love than can the individual psyche. And it is a Jewish lesson which you have learned only partially from books.

Of course this is only one story. There are many *d'rachim*, many paths to religious identification. This book is a mosaic of contributions from young spiritualists, artists, intellectuals, secularists, "Yiddishists," Zionists, scholars, radicals, rabbis. Each man's Jewish story is different. It is personal. Hopefully it is reflected, if not always explicitly addressed, in his writings.

Limits of time and space make this collection less than fully representative of a growing spectrum of Jewish concerns and commitments. Of each essay we can say that it describes an arena which has attracted the energies and enthusiasm of young American Jews in recent months.

Three of the essays (by Albert Axelrad, Raphael Arzt, and Everett Gendler) come from men somewhat older than the rest of the contributors, who are largely in their twenties. We have felt that it would be presumptuous to pretend that we have grown without the love and dedication of mentors, teachers, and guides. Rabbis Axelrad, Arzt, and Gendler are three such men; our debt to them and to scores of others can be but symbolically expressed by their participation in the creation of this book.

So this little volume is a collection of Jewish journeys, a portrait of personal translations of Jewish rootedness into modern life. As such it is the story of a small attempt to heal, to end spiritual famine, to find "gentle and joyous ways to be a man," perhaps through participation in a people or a community that strains the confines of time and space. In a sense, then, these essays carry the words of a whole generation in search of self and commitment. Their authorship, for the most part, is unmistakably that of young men trying to remain whole in a society which seems increasingly to deny the individual human vessel a sacred content and a communal setting. Our anger is that of people who wish not to be ripped asunder by graders, bureaucrats, organizational mentalities, and insane social priorities. Our passion is an attempt to create coalescing communities of trust and warmth. Our hope is not the hope of glib idealism, but of a tradition's long twilight struggle with reality and despair, handed down to us in all sobriety—or perhaps not without a discernible twinkle in the corner of the Jewish eye:

> The schools of Hillel and Shammai disputed two and a half years whether it would have been better if man had or had not been created. Finally they agreed that it would have been better had he not been created, but since he had been created, let him investigate his past doings, and let him examine what he is about to do. The meaning is, "Let him live a righteous life."
>
> —Talmud: Erub 13b

Can one really live passionately and conditionally at the same time? Some of the contributors to this volume walk that peculiarly Jewish tightrope. Their optimism seldom waxes utopian; their joy bubbles to the surface only upon occasion. But what is hopeful here is real, if fragile; it was not achieved by blinking the fact that humans are still brutally primitive in their perceptions and their actions and their evaluations.

Who are these "new Jews," products of paradox? How did they emerge among us? It is time to write a new chapter into a three thousand year story. Perhaps in so doing we are writing a bit of American history as well.

The Ghetto as Universe

The story of the new Jews begins with the point in time at which American society, Judaism, and the twentieth century first meet. It begins, simply, with the large scale immigration of their orthodox Jewish grandparents from the ghettos of Eastern Europe to American shores in the late nineteenth century.

In Europe the uniqueness and development of Judaism had been due in part to persecution. When one is an outcast from society, one is freed from some of the limitations and expectations that "first class citizens" hold for one another. Because they were set apart, the Jews could produce the Marxes, Freuds, Trotskys, and Einsteins, who enjoyed the outsider's perspective on the general society, and who could analyze and challenge social norms which were not wholly their own.

Most Jews, of course, chose not to challenge but to ignore their persecutors, and to turn unto themselves. It is this latter course of action which created the strong community of the ghetto, and which enriched Jewish life. For though he was an outsider in one world, the Jew was drawn to a center of gravity in another; indeed, he was often driven to it. Since the community of the ghetto was theocratic, it embraced his whole universe; self-contained, it could be warm and intense (and narrow) in a way that inhabitants of a secular republic may never come to understand. One did not abstract and correlate the facts of communal existence; one lived and savored them. The life of the peasant was to be uplifted and sanctified.

In a language that tries to capture that intensity, and

yet reflects the detachment and consequent nostalgia of the present, the following poem from a modern American edition of the high holiday prayerbook describes the famous *Kol Nidre* prayer:

> *Kol Nidre*—chant of ages,
> Chant of Israel, chant of sorrow,
> Measuring off the throbbing heartbeats
> Of a people bowed in anguish,
> Crushed by tyrants, thwarted, broken,
> Wandring ever; homeless, weary.
> Generations set your motif
> Out of trials, hopes and yearnings,
> Added each its variations
> To your theme and to your cadence.
> Diverse lands and diverse periods
> poured their souls into your music.
> When we hearken with our hearts tuned,
> We can hear the lamentations
> Through time's corridor resounding;
> We can see revealed before us
> Heroes, martyrs, saints and scholars,
> Loyal, steadfast sons of Israel,
> Sanctifying God, their Father.[1]

The Breaking of the Spheres: Transplant and Transition

That type of Judaism—like almost every form of all-inclusive community—is no more. As the pre-conditions of ghetto existence vanished, a new rationale for Jewish survival was needed. Hateful societies and violent pogroms which rent the ghetto asunder were only the catalysts of the old way's dissolution; the uneasy transplant of the ghetto which the Eastern European Jews tried to carry to America in the early twentieth century was foredoomed by more fundamental changes. In the wake of urbanization, Nietzsche, Science, and The Great War, the world which the Jews entered was itself adrift; as they were outcasts and refugees from their ghettos, so the West had been torn from its own traditional moorings.

But for most Jews, the new world was liberating and exhilarating. There was no time to evaluate and criticize a society which promised physical security and material success to anyone, regardless of his religion. Every day in every way the world was getting better; as American-born Jewish children were socialized into the general culture through the public schools and the business world, the ghetto community quietly dissolved.

The Jews played the new game well. In the flight from the inner cities to the more attractive residential districts, Judaism was forgotten, Jewishness rejected as inhibiting, disadvantageous, even shameful. But that rejection was often painful and seldom complete. Today many successful Jews, once violently resentful of their parents' orthodoxy, have made an uneasy peace with the past; they have discovered that their hostile or condescending attitude toward Jewish tradition is plagued with doubt and often overcome by nostalgia. For many, the riches of the new world have failed to satisfy; the warmth and piety of the old community are not found on Main Street or in Suburbia, and new substitutes are difficult to create. For some there is always the nagging suspicion that they are not really accepted, not completely "in" after all. Thus the emancipated, regardless of their irreligiosity, have tended to seek out their fellow Jews; in their new world country clubs and community centers and resorts they ape the larger society and remember the past.

But more than nostalgia and self-doubt have played a part in the "return to the synagogue." In the "better neighborhoods," the assimilating Jew learned that everyone, in order to be American, ought to have a religion and a house of worship. Paradoxically, in other words, acceptance of one's own roots, at least nominally, was a prerequisite for acceptance by a larger society; no one approved of the man who mocked his religion and had "nothing to pass on to his children."

Accordingly, Jewish suburbanites promptly and masterfully tailored an almost forgotten religion to the norms and aesthetics of middle-class culture. Houses of worship were made bigger and more modern than everyone else's. "Americanized" rabbis were to be hired by highly discriminating synagogue boards to bless their congregants' achievements, to consecrate the new way of life, to give time-honored meaning and legitimacy to putters, large lawns, and automobiles, and to present Judaism "properly" to benevolent ministers and curious neighbors.

Of course not everything about these developments was bad, nor do they reflect the entire spectrum of transition through which the Jewish community passed. Jewish schools and camps were supported in accordance with the famous corollary of the American pluralist myth that every child should "be exposed to his roots and heritage," and "know who he is." Parents' embarrassment at their inability to communicate this knowledge was joined to nostalgia and a healthy curiosity or search for new meaning; it resulted in enrollment in synagogue adult education programs, and in support of all kinds of Jewish cultural and religious institutions. In urban centers, strong and idealistic movements and organizations were founded. And the massive philanthropic efforts of the community are well known for the contributions they made to the quality of American life.

But we must notice that in all this activity there was a subtle shift, one which has not been lost upon the early children of suburbia, now in college: Judaism no longer was a driving moral force, the source of a way of life; it became an increasingly dispensable appendage of middle-class culture.

A Critique of the Transition:
Youth's Alienation

The American Jewish community is only beginning to come to terms with the meaning of this prostitution of Judaism to the status quo, and it is doing so because of the alienation of the majority of its young people. We have already suggested that their rejection of the Jewish community is less a denial of Judaism as such than it is part of a more general rejection of the deficiencies and misguided priorities inherent in the American Dream their parents have pursued. Judaism is rejected because it is seen as part and parcel of the hollow life-style, and because it has given young people no help in their search for alternatives to what has become the life-style of the Jewish suburb.

Few young people, after all, have any reason to believe that the wedding of Judaism and suburban life is not inevitable. They may know what the prophets said about those who can enjoy fine food, beautiful buildings, and the pleasantries of parties while a few miles away other human beings shiver and die. But they also know that almost every *Bar Mitzvah* boy is made to recite the words of those prophets in exchange for monetary gifts and an elaborate catered affair which is not served to people because they are hungry.

They know that the Jewish "ghettos" in the suburbs and finer residential city districts are not communities in the sense that the growing young need communities. Education there is streamlined, contrived, gutless. Even parental love often seems to respond to the child's performance as measured by limited standards (grades, "status") which are alien to the stimulation and celebration of deeper personal growth. So strong is the pressure to "perform" that Edgar Friedenberg has observed that, for all his piano lessons, scouting, foreign tours, and summer enrichment programs (all of which look good on "The Record"), the average high school graduate has never had the experience of creating by himself, assigning to himself, and then completing a major project or task of personal importance.

Jewish suburbia seems to some of us a creation of adults who overcame poverty and the sting of minority status by emphasizing the importance of "measuring up" to materialistic styles and performance-oriented standards as short-cuts to human dignity. Of course they "knew better," and it would be unfair to underestimate the well-intentioned sacrifice and real strength which were often expressed in the various achievements of suburban Jews. But we are concerned with the price that was paid in an often uncritical acceptance of "American life"; in slavishly imitating its trappings, these adults may have lost their capacity to challenge and affect its human and spiritual content.

So suburbia has been at once a launching pad and a target for the alienation and radicalism of the young—a launching pad because it has given them the affluence, sophistication, and perspective of Koheleth, and a target because it has furnished them with a microcosm of that society's bittersweet fruits, with the realization that affluence, sophistication, and perspective do not add up to Meaning.

It is no accident, then, that many radicals are those who "made it" in high school, and who used their superior talents and education to survey the opportunities open to them, only to conclude with student leader Mario Savio that

> The futures and careers for which young Americans prepare themselves are for the most part intellectual and moral wastelands . . . This chrome-plated consumers' paradise would have us grow up to be well-behaved children. . . .[2]

This unhappy critique, shared by thousands of young Jews languishing in suburban high schools, might appear to be a solipsistic luxury. But the broadened horizons of the college campus only suggest that the meaninglessness of home life reflects a more pervasive national disease. As he becomes aware of the plight of the poor and the cities, the college freshman concludes that his country's priorities subordinate human dignity to economic and military expansion. Yet, corporate profit and military power are as meaningless for a nation as wealth and status are for suburban parents. In the struggle of blacks and of radicals he detects not simply an attempt to extend these goals to the poor, but a deeper grasp at "soul," at a sense of community, at a way of life which speaks to his own unsatisfied personal and spiritual and creative needs. And, perhaps for the first time, he confronts the Jewish community as a group which has traded its soul and creativity for the power of consumption.

If the young person is sensitive and weak, he may drop out, withdraw, lapse into simplistic, intellectually barren (though often spiritually suggestive) commitments. If he is sensitive and strong, he may become a fighter, and hopefully a constructive builder of new communities. But weak or strong, responsible or not, he has come to share one of several popular versions of the suburban critique. At worst, he may feel that his parents, caught up in the consumers' paradise, see him as an extension of their struggle for status: if Johnny gets good grades and behaves, he is a good little status symbol; if not, he is a bad investment. Somewhat less harsh is the judgment of those who pity their parents, caught in a struggle they cannot escape, nostalgic for things they can no longer embrace. And of course the majority of young people—even of those who reject their elders' life-style—is more sympathetic: many know that their parents are good, principled people whose failings are neither entirely their fault nor irreversible.

Inevitably these critiques extend to the religious habits of the community: Judaism is seen as a benediction for the "system," as a hopeless longing for an irretrievable past, or as a repository of basically desirable values which cannot be implemented or taken seriously. Sometimes Jewish self-hatred prevents the more fruitful discovery of Judaism as a powerful and humanizing force, a source of moral imperatives and a personal guide toward lasting change.

Toward a New Synthesis

The sociological dictum that religion reflects its economic and social surroundings is not always valid. Because religions do draw upon traditions and imperatives which are not shaped by American life, because they claim to transcend current social arrangements, there is a constant tension, a dialectic of "push and pull."

In urban centers, young rabbis and educators kept alive another kind of Judaism, less molded by middle-class pressures, and capable, they felt, of offering an alternative way of life to the children of status seekers and organization men. They created summer camps and youth movements, seizing upon the renewed interest of the older generation in the synagogue. Sometimes their deep personal involvement with Jewishness fired their students with enthusiasm.

With the inauguration of these educational ventures has come a raging debate about the dubious ability of any teacher or counselor to mold Jews, to supply what early home experiences did not, to penetrate to the existential core of a young person with the emotional and intellectual "claims" of the past. Is it possible to confront the young future radical with the riches of a tradition that adds a unique form of spirituality and a vast reservoir of wisdom to the anguish of his critique of American life? Is this, indeed, a proper function for these camps and schools, or ought they to resign themselves to the less noble but seemingly more "practical" kind of holding action designed to keep young people within the Jewish fold under any circumstances?

Certainly the young cannot tolerate facile connections hastily made between Judaism and their most deeply felt problems and needs. Other aspects of youth culture, from the commune to the barricade, compete with the camps and schools for their attention and energies. Real living Jewish models, who can demonstrate what it is to see the world through Jewish eyes and through the passion of peoplehood, are in short supply; flannel boards and opaque projectors and trips to Israel do not make up the deficit.

Despite these handicaps, the new Jewish educators—through a process which should be the subject of more careful study—managed to nurture self-propelled young Jews in small numbers. Their creations—student magazines, newspapers, new schools and religious communities—have caught the imagination of many more young Jews than are actually involved in the groups. Those who have rediscovered the virtues of ethnicity through their radical or alienated social critiques have begun to converse seriously with those whose Jewish commitment is more firmly rooted in Jewish education. Workshops on "the Jewish arts" or on "Jewish radicalism" attract great numbers of Jews from an increasingly broad spectrum of religious and political orientations. Magazines like *Response* (which has printed several of the essays in this volume) have become clearing houses for the sharing of information, ideas, and critiques.

Thus a growing and fluid community of young people who are serious about Judaism has become visible in this country during the past two or three years. Wooed by the survival-minded Jewish establishment, while at the same time scorned by other traditional vested interests, these new Jewish groups are suggesting to an entire generation that Judaism may be community-oriented and activist as well as middle-class and congregational—that in fact the Jewish soul is probably more at home in the former role.

The Jewish Paradox Restored

The "new Jews" do not pretend that Judaism is of such universal theoretical applicability as to have "answers" to modern problems. I have tried to suggest that to see the world through Jewish eyes in this century is to embrace a paradox of hope and despair; to support the anguish of alienation with the strength of a mighty untapped reservoir of resources for personal identity and moral involvement as well as with a language of aesthetics and a way to express personal spiritual development which offers new perspectives to American youth.

The productive union of Jewish life and the radical's grasp for answers is not always an easy one to effect, of course. On the social front the religious and activist communities have much in common: both argue that the "human dimension" must be brought into societal decision-making, both are passionately concerned with justice. But the religious community is more explicitly concerned with nurturing the vision and personal depth which should lie behind the public decisions and strategies of the activist; as such it may have more "territory behind the lines," and its membership and emphasis may be different. The Jewish activist confronts the broad spectrum of human suffering and struggle and sees his small interactive community as an ultimate building-block of humanity; his political activities are supplemented by his concern for the intensity, the depth, and the sensitivity of his own microcosmic community. At times it is a difficult balance of energies and perspectives.

Ultimately I suspect that there is more that is attractive in this synthesis of the universal and the particular than the "healthy creative tension" that may result. Ethnicity and particularism are more than expedients; we cannot escape the knowledge that, whatever Judaism may be for us today, it owes its survival to the belief of our ancestors that Israel somehow transcends the historical contexts through which it wends its paradox-ridden way. It is not clear that Jewishness makes any sense when its sociological roots have been summed, and when its achievements have been behaviorally, historically, and philosophically analyzed. The ultimate claim to a tie with spiritual dimensions of experience which eludes our rational inquiry stares at us constantly through the pages of our history. It is to be hoped that, whatever the specifics of his theology, the Jew will not be able to remain insensitive to the sense of ultimacy and mystery which enters all of our lives and is the spinal cord of our people's past.

Beyond the Pale

We Americans live in an age when society makes heavy demands upon our time, energies, and perceptions of reality. Mesmerized by personal concerns, caught in the momentum of striving after goals whose validity we lack the strength, perspective, or freedom to question, we nevertheless sense our lack of faith, and catch occasional glimpses of a social monster flirting with self-destruction, whether in ecological upset, political polarization and civil war, nuclear holocaust, or moral collapse and collective mental breakdown. Great are the pressures which prevent us from shaking ourselves free, from constructing new loci of human interaction and faith. Awesomely obscure are the true reins of social power, the levers which quicken justice. Once again, as perhaps in every time of rapid change, apocalypse seems to loom larger than ever before.

So perhaps it is not presumptuous to suggest that the fate of the new Jews' attempt to overcome alienation and despair is of significance beyond the Jewish pale. American youth stands at a new frontier: we have been the beneficiaries and the victims of the old American Dream of material comfort and open opportunity; now, a frightening and exciting world of intangible goals and human redefinition beckons, even as we are pressured by a spiritually hollow society to ignore its call. Our alienation and radical activity—and our sigh—is a suggestion that we are only beginners in that new world, unable any longer to bear the confines of the old. Perhaps that has always been the story of the Jew.

NOTES

Frontispiece: Martin Buber, *Hasidism and Modern Man*, Maurice Friedman, trans. and ed., New York: Harper and Row, 1966, p. 57.

1. Morris Silverman, ed., United Synagogue of America, *High Holiday Prayerbook*, Hartford: Prayer Book Press, 1961, p. 208.
2. Mario Savio, "An End to History," *The New Student Left*, Boston: Beacon Press, 1967, p. 252.

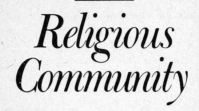

Part One

Religious
Community

The term havurah *means religious fellowship, and is classically used to describe groups of pietists and mystics which emerged in the first century A.D. and in the Middle Ages. The term now applies to several experimental religious communities, most notably in Boston and New York City. The* havurot *are comprised of young Jews, usually of graduate school age, both single and married. The first group was founded in September 1968, in Boston; the second in New York approximately a year later. Although they do not necessarily live together, members of the* havurot *join one another often for religious study, experimental worship, experiencing of the Sabbath, communal meals and retreats, and political action. The attempt is to create a small authentic Jewish community, the most important bases of which are interpersonal understanding and serious commitment to the confrontation of religious and moral issues and experiences. The* havurot, *by their very existence, constitute an indictment of and a turning away from the traditional American Jewish community.*

Small communities are often hesitant to describe themselves; their self-conscious identities are always in flux. But in the piece that follows, Alan Mintz discusses the forces and feelings that led up to the establishment of the havurot, *and suggests, at least in part, what they hope to achieve. His approach is personal and describes his own experiences in the secular culture, experiences which led him to participation in the* havurah. *He also sketches his personal understanding of the nature of Judaism, and tells why he feels this experimental Jewish community to be so important.*

Along the Path to Religious Community[*]

by ALAN MINTZ

I

I am a religious communitarian. I am interested in small fellowships of Jews who study, worship, and act together in a setting of interpersonal understanding. I am a member of the *Havurah* in New York City.

Such is my identity in programmatic terms. The subject here, however, is not program but rather the roots of the commitment—that is, how, in a very subjective fashion, I arrived at this identity.

In presenting sources, reasons, and the decision, one is forced to become somewhat schematic and fragmentary. The burden of my remarks will be two lists: first, those dissatisfactions with general and campus culture which have led me to search for alternative experiences, and sec-

[*] This selection originally appeared in *Midstream*, Vol. XVI, No. 3, March 1970.

ond, those discoveries about Judaism which have made it attractive as a locus of activity.

1. *The Designification of Action*   One of the noticeable features of campus protest is its symbolic nature. One protests military recruiting on campus and dealings with firms that produce immoral weapons, but not the war itself. This is necessary because we have no power to affect the war, so we must, out of desperation, make gestures which are increasingly symbolic and removed from the war. The less our acts impinge on the world, the more we perform them principally to confirm our own identities and self-definitions. We begin to share Camus's assumption of absurdity and to believe that his account of Sisyphus' continual rolling up of the ever backsliding rock indicates the stance we must adopt. We then see the world—that which is outside our own subjectivity—as given, determined, in the hands of immense and arbitrary historical forces. And if one indeed does address American society on its macrocosmic level, one must think along these lines and must see only private, subjective value in one's actions.

For many of us, this path is only existentialism's way of rationalizing our impotence. If what we say and do does not matter, then we cannot care about what we say, or even feel motivated to act at all. We reject this nothingness not in a willing game of self-delusion, but in the belief that we can carve out for ourselves island-worlds in which the effect of our acts will be felt. We withdraw our energies—at least directly—from addressing pathetically and symbolically centers of immense power; we seek to find pockets of meaning on whose creation and becoming we can leave some mark. We need to be in some creative relation to our future.

2. The Fragmentation of Community   For any Jew today, including the Israeli, who decides to live in some open relation to the world, the tension of living in two civilizations is alternatingly enriching and lacerating, but always interminable and inescapable. Such is one's condition, the given of existence, the nature of things. The ambiguous insights of the secular present and the demands of the Jewish past are thesis and antithesis which will not be dissolved in a comfortable synthesis. The selfhood of the young Jew today must, consequently, be so defined; he cannot expect to exist in a milieu in which his full person can be actualized and exposed, but must accept the realities of fragmentation and compartmentalization. He chooses one group for his political involvement, another for his intellectual growth, another for his religious practice, still another for spiritual search, and so on. . . . To each group he presents an encapsulated aspect of himself to be shared; nowhere must he expect fully to reveal himself.

The emerging concept of decentralized fellowship seeks not to avoid the tensions of living in secular society but rather to create a milieu in which Jews can grapple together with a shared appreciation of struggle, a base from which to look outward on the world. That is, a setting where personal relations can be formed, based on the knowledge of the full person, where being rather than performance is encouraged. Here, hopefully, the sparks of self-integration and group trust might begin to be regathered.

3. The Middle-Class Ethos   It is, of course, indisputable that well-off Jewish middle-class society has bequeathed valuable norms to its children: strong family bonds, generous financial giving, concern for education, steadfastness in accomplishing communal goals, etc. The evils of this society are made all the more dangerous and insinuating because they are the perversions and excesses of these same virtues; positive traits become ugly and defensive in reaction to the general American society.

A. OBSESSION WITH PERFORMANCE. The genuine concern for learning and culture which existed has been transmuted into an obsession with performance in school and before other audiences. Achievement and intellect exist only as commodities defined by the school, artistic sensitivity only as its display confirms the parents' success as parents. "Let my son play something for you" belies something more insidious than motherly pride. Moreover, education can only be measured by achievement in school, not by the presence of intellectual curiosity, critical instinct, creativity, or any characteristic through which the development of the child might be unfolded. This would not be so bad if Jewish middle-class society did not hold performance as nearly the only standard of judging the child's worth. Who doesn't know many smart people who, as children, because they could not be *brilliant* in school, deliberately began to fail, then to lie in order to avoid the anxiety of being discovered, and so on? Who doesn't know men who carry throughout their adulthood a suspicion of their own worth on this account; women who could only see themselves marrying "professional types"; people whose ability to enjoy themselves is mitigated by vestiges of the "only-if-it-doesn't-interfere-with-your-school-work" ethos?

B. OVERPROTECTIVENESS. One of the major tragedies of Jewish child-rearing is the isolation of adolescents one from another at a period when the family ceases to affect their values and to be able to hold them by power alone. At this time, contact with other kids is of inestimable importance, as is exposure to alternative adult models, ones more idealistic than the parents. Many adults, stunted in their development and afraid in their personal relations, could have worked out their problems in adolescence if familial protection had been relaxed enough to allow them to spend more time in a supervised setting with other teenagers. If more daughters had been freed for such exposure there would not be so many women who consider themselves primarily princesses.

C. SUPPRESSION OF THE EMOTIONS. Jewish middle-class life possesses no language of the emotions, no words to express subtleties of feeling, no freedom from self-consciousness. Where there are no exterior symbols to express interior states, the latter disappear also. If this is the classic plight of Western bourgeoisie, the Jews have done little that is exemplary to make things better. We have nowhere to look for release from the oppressive dullness and standardization of feeling, no chance for breakthrough into occasional joy and reverie. Even the natural expression of anger has been contained in my generation in favor of artificial politeness and even-temperedness. One can only wonder, when such an elemental emotion has been driven underground to brood in black interiors, in what perverted forms it will reappear.

4. *The Desanctification of Experience* Life events devoid of spirituality, the slithering by of time unpunctuated by holy moments, process without periodic disengagement for overview and resentment, physical acts which fail to point beyond themselves, and the delusion of genuine love in diffuse lovingness—such is the fluid in which we seem inescapably immersed. Even the few extant illuminati think they constitute a new phenomenon and avoid encountering models of past religiosity through which they might enrich and refine themselves. Generally, the reductivist thrust of positivism and scientism annihilates the possibility of symbolic ambiguity; the mass media make all language suspect. Those moments of special meaning that we indeed experience are isolated and accidental oc-

currences in an otherwise meaningless style of life, nor are
we able to create a ground for their more frequent occurring. Even the culture in which many of us exist, academia
and the intellectual world, drowns out the spiritual with
its self-confident humanism. We have nowhere to look for
models, for *rebbes* who are involved in the world but not
imprisoned by it, and who seriously seek religious knowledge but are not enslaved by scholasticism and legalism.

5. *The Bankruptcy of Study*   I studied at Columbia College as an undergraduate and on occasion encountered
some very good teaching, as good as one can probably find
around. None of these courses, however, began to be an
experience of rich personal and moral activity. At best,
ideas were explained subtly and lucidly; the "world" of the
text was fully grasped, its assumptions laid bare, its implications stated. In the "learning" process, the intellect was
regarded as the supreme arbiter of things and given full
play. The possibility that intellectuality, that ideas were
not the only possible level on which to learn was never
admitted by the academy. I did not find there the desire to
dwell in the realm of value, belief, personal decision, and
personal dialectic with the world of the text through
which the student works at creating himself and in the
process exposes himself to others. The refusal to entertain
the middle ground between the twin dangers of intellectuality and group therapy must mean the sterilization of
study, the transformation of knowledge into a commodity.

II

Although I have never been distant from Judaism in my
activity and personal observance, my involvement has recently been illuminated by a series of new realizations
which make me very happy about possibilities of the future. Although I shall speak of "discoveries," these matters

have been implicit all along. It seems, however, that American Jewish culture, having absorbed the worst of Americanism and the most insipid of Judaism, has conspired to keep these realizations from me in my upbringing and Jewish education, which textually was among the better to be had. A shift in consciousness in the past few years has fortunately allowed many young Jews to participate in a sense of a renewed possibility of personal ties with Judaism. What has amounted to a transvaluation has enabled many to conceive of Judaism once more in images of vitality and richness. My own realizations about Judaism run along the following lines.

1. Root Identity   When I came to school, I was impatient with my limited exposure to the world and was eager for radically new experiences. I wanted my life decisions and identity formation to be undertaken out of choice and knowledge rather than ignorance and desperation. It was very important for me then to discover that Jewishness was an irrevocable element in the defining of my being, that my differentness and particularity were part of my condition, givens in my existence. The awareness was different from ethnic pride or the newly fashionable particularism; rather, it constituted the degree zero, the point of departure for the consideration of entry into religious style, communal association, and historical process.

Why? Perhaps the way I was raised, perhaps my Jewish education, perhaps the polarized world of "them" and "us" into which I was socialized very early. But certainly as of late the consciousness of the holocaust has been decisive; the almost metaphysical necessity of my particularity, the indelible nature of my uniqueness have jolted me, and I have come to aver that my lot is with the Jews. What happens to them, happens to me.

But please note that for many this realization is identical with survivalism: the commandment that after Auschwitz a Jew remain a Jew, and the Jews remain a people. If the discussion remains on this level, there is nothing here for me more than regressive minimalism, an increasingly defensive posture which seeks to preserve Judaism as she is and Jewish institutions as they are. That is not my fight. The phrase "what happens to the Jews" does not mean to me "what the world does to the Jews and how they react" but rather "what kind of community the Jews build for themselves, what quality of existence they will choose." The imperative is not to survive in the aftermath of destruction but to create a vital and just future out of the extraordinary materials offered us.

If this is the case, we must turn inward toward Judaism and the Jewish community as the stage on which to play out our social and religious aspirations. One does not like the Jewish community, but one feels responsible for what it becomes. Three areas of action become apparent: sensitizing the community to the social dilemmas of our time and helping to formulate a religiously-based response; criticizing and attacking institutions and demanding they conform more closely to Jewish values; and most importantly, constituting as many uncompromised counter or parallel institutions as possible. We seek not defense of the community but participation in its becoming.

2. *A Fuller Past*   A most startling discovery has been that Judaism does not have to be identical to the scheme of middle-class values. Even though the two are taken as the same entity today, the equation is not determined and necessary. A new consciousness of the past has brought us to believe that a more fundamental and nourishing Judaism existed, was discussed, and did not need a middle-class life-style and its constellation of values.

The United States has up to now read its past as a series of consecrated values current at the time and, by so doing, has been blind to entire sections of its history. Similarly, the Jewish community has persuaded us to believe that certain periods and tendencies in our history constitute the sources of what is "normatively" and "legitimately" Jewish. Our discovery has been that the Jewish past is pluralistic and multi-traditional, and that no degree of institutional power can label one period or one tradition as *the* source of legitimate Judaism. We now begin the scrutiny of that which was either kept from us or despised as deviant: mysticism, sectarianism, Hasidism, liturgy, religious poetry, the traditions of non-violence and sensuality, the *gemeindschaft* of *shtetl* (small community) life, the Holocaust, and many other areas.

Why have Torah and Halacha (Jewish law) been excluded from the list? Because here our discovery has not been of their existence but of their contemporary meaning. Torah and *mitzvot* (biblical commandments) constitute in our lives the demanding Other, the qualifying presence which commands us to transcend in deeds what is natural and gratifying for us. Torah is the crucial component of the religious scheme which respects but does not indulge the subject.

3. *Politics and Shabbat* I locate myself in Judaism because I find it is fertile to both social striving and spiritual growth; because I find both possibilities symbiotically contained in the performance of the *mitzvot;* because as we recover lost segments of our past and refurbish old models I can feel sincerely grounded in Judaism; because I need a past with which to interrogate and be interrogated; because I want to demonstrate politically and experience *Shabbat* with the same people; and because my *neshama,* my soul, cannot be refined and do right without the community.

III

I have discussed the roots of my commitment, I have talked of needs, pressures, and discoveries rather than programs, projects, and projections. I wish to add a note about these latter categories. I mean by the term religious communitarianism a tissue of independent communities which might be described in this manner: small groups of persons involved in the creating and determining of their communal becoming, who do not necessarily live together but interrelate as whole persons, who aid each other in the growth and actualization of each, who study the Jewish past and draw from its riches in creating their own individual and communal religious patterns, who turn to the world and act on its stage for the realization of Torah, who celebrate together individual and historical moments of joy and sorrow, who are not afraid to expose their children to other adults as non-parental examples, who *daven* together and seek new songs to sing to God, who seek to reestablish ties with the natural world, and who, in the future, will be able to say, "May we be proud of the work of our hands."

In Preparation for a Jewish
Radical Politics

Many of the young Jews whose activities and interests are represented in this book are dissatisfied with the ideological and ahistorical ethos of much of recent American student radicalism. For some of us, Jewish life contributes important additional arenas and dimensions to the expression of our radical commitments, drawing as it does upon the historical perspective, particularism, and religious genius of a people and a civilization whose experience spans many centuries.

In the following two essays, Robert Greenblatt and James Sleeper sketch some of the outlines of their critiques of current radical movements; they indicate, as well, what some of those additional dimensions are which Judaism can contribute to the struggles for liberation that characterize our time.

Robert Greenblatt, a founding co-chairman of the Student Mobilization Committee to End the War (MOBE), argues that the American Jewish community, by embracing the universality of the American melting-pot myth, has forsaken the truly unique and radical components of Jewish tradition which might make that tradition a significant contributor to the advancement of life and liberty in our society. He suggests that the sweeping universalism which has engulfed both assimilationists and radicals alike is of questionable value to the American future, and he points toward basic changes in American Jewish life which must precede the community's re-entry into the prophetic role.

Robert was born in Hungary in 1938, and spent the war in a concentration camp. In this country, he attended Brooklyn College, Yale, and Cornell, where he received a Ph.D. in mathematics.

James Sleeper suggests that radicalism which has lost its capacity to affirm as well as to oppose becomes impotent as a force for lasting change; he suggests that in their unresponsiveness to the spiritual and the deeply interpersonal realms of human experience—and to history's contributions to these categories—some radicals reflect their victimization by the very society whose immorality, dehumanization, and idolatry they

35

reject. Glib references to love, peace, and human dignity do not constitute meaningful affirmation, nor do they provide the bases for a positive, loving, and peaceful style of life.

These essays call for a reintegration, by young Jews, of the lasting historical and spiritual perspectives which can inform a meaningful and humanizing radicalism; they argue that participation in and identification with the Jewish experience is a means through which that reintegration can proceed.

Out of the Melting Pot,
Into the Fire

---

by ROBERT GREENBLATT

We are surrounded by the explosions of discontent and
fear, resulting from long-term exploitation and neglect.
The myths of the past, used to camouflage oppressive racial and class structures, are disintegrating faster than new
ones can be erected in their place. Political nostrums, social science jargon and rehashed ideological rhetoric
about equality and opportunity continue to be hawked on
the television street corner of America, but they seem only
vaguely related to the events around us. Unreal leaders in
electronic boxes appear before us as little gray manne-
quins, speaking into the wind words they have not written
to people they cannot see about problems they do not
know. And the Great American Experiment seems to be
coming down all around us, without rhyme or reason, like
the deacon's masterpiece, that wonderful one-horse shay

which ". . . went to pieces all at once/ All at once and nothing first/ Just as bubbles do when they burst."

But the reasons are here, have always been here, beneath the layers of myths and illusions and rationalizations, laborious constructions intended as substitutes for the unifying and stabilizing collective unconscious built up by older nations over many centuries of history but serving instead to obscure the inequities of Amerika and consuming in the process the available energy needed to construct a just society.

The myths changed and grew ever more grandiose with each new need for rationalization. The frontier spirit and self-reliance, manifest destiny, laissez faire, free enterprise and the great melting pot: these are the tombstones of a people enslaved, another exterminated and the waves of immigrants neglected, exploited and digested. But some of the victims refuse to die. And as they begin to stir, shaking the foundations of a society built upon their premature graves, we find the cracks and fissures everywhere, breaking through the plaster of egalitarian myths, exposing the truly stabilizing factors: the interdependence of parasitic relationships, the vested interests of the middle class and the coercive power of the state controlled by a corporate ruling elite. Societies and men have ever been mesmerized by such exploitive myths, not only because of their charismatic force but because of the primacy of man's social character. Contrary to Genesis I, men antedate Man and society precedes Adam and Eve. The act of creation, despite our subsequent pretensions, was the collective act of some primeval ape society emerging into a new life struggle. Only the collective nature of the act provided the conditions for survival and regeneration. But this same collective consciousness makes us easy prey for mythmakers.

It is a descriptive fact, and not an adverse judgment, that consciousness of the species as a whole is a necessary

pre-condition for the development of the consciousness of
the individual self. It is part of the basic earth upon which
our feet are planted, regardless of where our minds soar,
and was so recognized long before Jung wrote about the
collective unconscious. The earliest dialogues of the Tal-
mudists, those profound revisionists of religious and political orthodoxy, alluded to it not only by suggesting that all
souls of future generations resided in Adam, but by postu-
lating additional children of the first couple, never mentioned in Genesis.

The American melting pot idea, while it lasted, was
one of the more imaginative among the exploitive myths
of history. And the Jews, because of the peculiarity of a
collective psyche forged in diaspora, were especially vulnerable to its lure. The appeal of the melting pot for Jews
lay not only in its egalitarian trappings but in the promise,
so rhapsodically put by Emma Lazarus, to re-admit into
the species the most isolated, battered and desperate
members of humanity.

Despite occasional revolutionary movements like the
Bundists, the diaspora promoted Jewish consciousness of
permanent transience, reinforced by historical reality and
sustained by other-worldliness or messianic allusions to
Zion. It acted as a powerful deterrent to the full integration of the Jews as a total community into the social and
political struggles of the ambient culture. Individuals
caught up in both worlds continually faced the limitations
of two unpalatable choices: chauvinism or *luftmentshkeit*.
America is succeeding where Spain and Germany failed—
whole communities of American Jews have become like
relapsing Marranos, Christian in the day time, slipping
into our basements at night to worship Jewish symbols,
the meaning and content of which have been lost in antiquity.

During its period of credibility, the melting pot served
as the contractual mechanism for buying into American

democracy and affluence and was rarely recognized as a device for fragmentation and mass control. Just enough ethnic and cultural variety was permitted to disarm the wary, to separate us into mutually hostile, competitive groups and to keep us vulnerable to collective blackmail. Not nearly enough identity was allowed to remain to serve as a source of moral inspiration or political strength and unity, capable of providing motivation, energy and power for progressive action. For the nub of the paradox is that if unifying myths are essential to stabilize societies, control and rule people and maintain the status quo, then unity among people is all the more essential to change societies, break the yoke of control and transform the status quo.

But the myths of the melting pot, America's plastic substitute for the rich experience of peoplehood, have been destroyed beyond salvage by the recent movement of Black and Third World peoples, to whom this co-optative and castrating elixir was never made available, for they were not merely outcasts, but to be regarded as a different species. Those non-white peoples, whom history exempted from this trap by never making it available, are now being cajoled and coerced into it through the co-optative mechanisms of such programs as Black capitalism and repressive cultural nationalism. And, as in every previous case, the efficacy of this approach rests on successful recruitment of ethnic collaborators willing to help transform the peculiar cultural and normative energies of the group into enslaving and alienating functions. Indeed, the share of relative affluence and apparent autonomy permitted to any group in America tends to be in direct proportion to the extent to which it has succeeded in internalizing these repressive functions. The pitifully small minority who escaped, largely by their own efforts, and adopted inter-ethnic and international perspectives, are hounded as anarchists or foreign agents by the state and as traitors by the various ethnic *mafiosi*.

The issues and events which, we are told, are tearing America apart, are merely bringing into the open the elaborate subterranean network of antagonisms and hostilities used to manipulate and control us. But, if the rising of Third World peoples in America and around the world has exposed anew the reactionary forces of national, ethnic and racial consciousness, it has also brought to light the revolutionary possibilities buried in and, at times, retrievable from vague cultural memories and almost instinctive group loyalties, long misused and corrupted. A number of small but possibly significant movements have thus been inspired, notably among "radical" Catholics and some "young" Jews. For many, these movements are based on the subjective reality of those memories and loyalties and on the premise that 1) reconstruction, even revolution, were once primary and are still latent in their own cultural, ethnic or religious heritage (indeed, it was precisely the great and repeated historic sell-outs, misdirection and manipulation of these energies into sectarian and chauvinistic channels which made them useful as reactionary instrumentalities); and 2) that this, combined with the ability openly to confront reality and the willingness to act out the consequences dictated by the combination of these two, will contribute elements essential both to constructing the vision of what America should be and to the process of bringing it about. The validity of the premises can be tested only by history. Their plausibility, however, can and must be examined more closely.

Buried in the memories of our cultural past are principles often still too radical to appear as demands by the most militant of groups, but rarely are they taught in Jewish educational institutions: land reform and redistribution of

wealth and protections against self-incrimination that
make the Bill of Rights appear like rules of procedure for a
Star Chamber. The injunction from Ethics of the Fathers
to "make a fence around the Torah" and to guard and preserve ethical and social precepts has been bartered away
in substance in our opportunistic desire to "become like
the other nations of the world." We have traded it for the
maxim of Robert Frost's thoughtless and superstitious
farmer: Good fences make good neighbors. We erect and
maintain institutions which separate us from our neighbors and destroy the values the fences are supposed to
preserve.

The tradition of Abraham at Sodom and Gomorrah established the obligation to struggle on behalf of all people,
even if it means challenging highest authority. Jonah
was reprimanded and punished for refusing to preach to
Nineveh, not Jerusalem. We have allowed this tradition to
degenerate into an almost empty practice. We appoint
Shabbas goyim, a few individual or institutional Jewish
spokesmen who make eloquent civil rights speeches and
pressure for insignificant reforms through "proper channels," while the bulk of our community is indifferent to or
mobilizes against the aspirations and demands of oppressed people in our midst. From the grandeur and courage of Abraham we have come to the infamy of hate-filled
Jewish vigilante groups and the New York City teachers'
strike. The very purpose and concept of education, the desire for learning we pride ourselves on, has become one
more salable product in the market place. When discussing the effect of the "Jewish Revival 1940-1956," Nathan
Glazer gives this account in his volume *American Judaism:*

> The economic advantages that had been built up in pre-
> vious years, even during the hard years of the depres-

sion, in the form of superior education and experience in business bore fruit in the years of prosperity, and American Jews became an extremely prosperous group, probably as prosperous as some of the oldest and longest established elements of the population of the United States.

Statistical studies of the economic position of Jews in America render this comment more striking. In 1946, for example, according to the Gallup Poll, almost sixty percent of American Jews were in business or executive and professional positions, and the figure goes above eighty-one percent if white-collar jobs are included, with less than two percent in the service and laborer categories.

Jews, almost more than any other group, have integrated the economic, social and political values of American capitalism and have made themselves dependent on its stability and continuity. The melting pot, that orderly ladder of progression which Jews so proudly and mistakenly climbed, continues to function as support for the levels presently achieved, but only if the lower rungs continue to exist. Consolidation of past gains and prospects for further advancement are contingent on the continued existence of a massive lower class and under class. This is the resolution of the paradox of liberal Jews and Jewish institutions now at odds with the impatient demands of the poor and the disenfranchised. For the civil rights fight for equal opportunity was, first and foremost, a battle to preserve the ladder as the legitimate and universal method of advancement, whereas the more militant struggles of the present, objectively anti-capitalist in nature even when projecting apparently reformist programs, challenge the legitimacy, and hence the stability, of the ladder itself. Therefore, not only the poor and oppressed, but young Jews who, out of the depths of their heritage, join in the liberation struggles of growing power and momentum, too often come up against their former allies across the barricades.

While still reciting the liberal pieties, Jews move out of the center city as fast as any redneck. Men and women, progressives and even radicals whose consciences turned them to teaching and social work in the thirties, have become blind and self-serving bureaucrats, victims and victimizers in a system which gives to one only what it takes from another. The once proud edifices of Jewishly financed non-sectarian philanthropic institutions, hospitals and settlement houses have become the mausoleums in which are entombed the dignity and aspirations of Blacks, Puerto Ricans, Chicanos and others. Meanwhile, our sensitivity is turning into cynicism, our wisdom to patronization and our pride to xenophobia.

American Jews are functioning reflexively in a time of crisis and without discernible communal purpose. The traditional answer of the diaspora (exile outside Israel), that we are a people in search and waiting for a homeland, is a useless rationale for those millions who want to remain Jews and do not plan to "return." Nor can American Jews be merely expatriate Israelis, functioning as a community only to give uncritical support to Israeli policies, contributing to the UJA and apologizing for American imperialism in exchange for military aid.

Required is a different approach to the problems of diaspora, an approach which accepts, after all these centuries, the obvious proposition that diaspora is not a temporary condition. It should be no surprise that this approach is not new, implicit as it is in the traditional view that there can be no return to Zion before the messianic age, a millennium in which all the world is to participate.

While the economic position and present political consciousness of American Jews do not make adoption of such a course seem likely, our history and culture contain the ingredients for such development. And the alternatives are neither numerous nor enticing: assimilation, emigration or continued dependence on the efficacy of counter-revolution.

The last third of the twentieth century promises to be a period of unprecedented ferment, due to the worldwide quest and determination for economic, political and cultural emancipation. Institutions and philosophies will be measured harshly in the context of this quest. The fate of Israel, for example, will be decided by the role of her people in the social revolutionary movement which is sure to engulf the Middle East, not by diplomatic deals of nation-states or the fervent but shortsighted loyalty of world Jewry. American Jews will have to define themselves primarily in relation to the ongoing struggle to restructure America. Our communal purpose and (peoplehood) will emerge in the midst of this struggle, or not at all.

The demands placed on us are as ancient as our history: *Na'aseh V' nishmah.* A statement not of blind faith but of uncompromising dedication and idealism: we will do what is right and take whatever the consequences. We must take full part in the coming and necessary American revolution as followers and leaders, as communities and individuals. We must do this on the side of the oppressed because it is right and it, too, is our heritage. We must reorient our relation to the past, cease using it as justification of the inequities of the present and the method for predetermining and freezing the future. Rather, the past must provide roots for the present and strength to change the future.

We will never be "like the other nations" unless thousands of years of history can be erased or willed away. Our past survival as a people was not tied to any piece of land,

and a realistic contemplation of the future must begin with that fact. If survival is our fate, one hundred years hence the world will undoubtedly witness a Jewish minority even in Israel, a minority whose kinship to Israelis will be based on common ancestry, not common prophetic vision.

The continuation of every human institution must ultimately be based on its ability to serve the people. The continued survival of Jewish peoplehood, as distinct from the survival of individual Jews, will not escape this test. For this reason, the question of the Jews' survival as a people is inextricably bound up with the role played by Jewish communities in the social and political struggles surrounding them. A major part of the answer to the question of survival will be determined in America.

The possibilities are challenging and difficult, but very real. The coming and necessary American revolution will be chaotic and unprecedented for all the participants, not least because of the apparent absence of the unifying factors necessary to transform rebellions into revolution. In such a setting, every cohesive social force must be examined for its potential as a source of energy and solidarity.

The experiences of Vietnam and Cuba have demonstrated the possibility of revolutionary nationalism, a consciousness of peoplehood which contributes to the revolutionary process while maintaining an international perspective. The emerging character of Third World movements in America reinforce this possibility and point out a direction for a new generation of American Jews.

It is not difficult to draw parallels between our present situation and the ancient period of bondage under the Pharaohs. As before, we must reject privilege accumulated on the backs of slaves, physical and spiritual, and embark on a course of struggle. And as before, the hope is placed in the young, the new Jews born in the struggle and not yet corrupted by Baal or Mammon, for only they will survive the long march through the desert. One new factor is the lesson which the failure of the original Exodus has tried to teach us over these thousands of years of diaspora: we cannot go somewhere else for our liberation and we cannot be liberated alone.

I am a Jew, an American, a Revolutionary. I am all three at once because each flows out of and merges into one life history. I continue to be each one by choice and self-definition, as well as external, but in no case universal, judgment. Establishment of my claim to each of these honorifics was accompanied by hardship and fulfillment, in the ghettos and camps of Europe, as an immigrant in America and in the streets and jails and under the night-sticks of this "golden land." I seek neither dialogue nor accommodation with the soured and hate-filled scraps of humanity who deny my claim to be a Jew, an American, a Revolutionary unless I denounce all but one. But to those sisters and brothers who honestly question the compatibility of these categories, I declare my belief that the synthesis is a necessary pre-condition and must therefore be a part of our revolutionary vision.

The Case for
Religious Radicalism[*]

by JAMES A. SLEEPER

Now and again, as I consider the priorities and values
which govern my activities and those of others around me,
I am confronted with the discovery that there are many
ways of being alive, many levels of experience, many com-
binations of spirituality, intellect, and emotion, intuition,
reason, myth, and concrete structure through which a man
might happily live his life. The Government of the United
States appears to be the willing servant and guarantor of a
shockingly narrow range of these possibilities.

By now we are all familiar with the proposition that
ours is a society whose goals are for the large part economic. And we know that the pursuit of material wealth
and status, corporate power and national pride carries
with it the seeds of many tragedies. These are narrow

[*] This selection originally appeared in *Genesis II*, Vol. 1, No. 2, March
1970.

goals, after all; one wonders whether they admit of awe or reverence. For communion in human relationships, economics seems to substitute transaction; for celebration it substitutes construction; for myth and symbol it offers machine and system. The image of man, and the standards by which we measure the quality of his life, as they emerge from the particular culture that has been described as "American," are increasingly frightening to me.

To experience these feelings—not simply to expound them but rather to sense them in both national event and personal situation—is to begin to enter into a radical critique of one's society. The liberal's faith in the democratic workings of the system is no longer satisfying, because politics within the established processes are merely ways of seeing that everyone—regardless of race, religion, or creed—receives his "fair share" of the American social pie. But what if the pie is poisonous? One begins to become a radical when one discovers that liberals can handle quantitative demands for a redistribution of the pie but *not* qualitative demands for a change in its recipe. Am I quite sure that I want the black man to get his "fair share"? Indeed, perhaps the only reason he has "soul" is because he's been fortunate enough *not* to get it. And perhaps the reason the American Jewish community is so antiseptic and soulless is that it has bitten off more than it can chew.

But to say that the American social pie is poisonous, that it contains a narrow range of the possible human and spiritual ingredients, and in dangerously warped proportions, is only the beginning of radicalism. Having rejected one diet as nauseating, I must have something else to eat. Here begins my quarrel with many of my radical friends; they are not good cooks.

Let us grant even the most sweeping of critiques; let's grant for the moment that we really *have* reached the brink of apocalypse in this country; this is mankind's last, best chance, says the radical, and we've just about blown it. And let's assume that we've refuted and dismissed the patronizing criticisms of radicals by psychologists who tell us of our personal tensions rather than of the society which aggravates them. Let's even agree that 1984 is so much here that most of us don't even know it; that we've been mesmerized into consumer-robots seeking physical need-gratification at the expense of a deeper consciousness and love.

Let us grant that in the absence of myth and community, a mechanical collectivity whose only cohesion is monetary has brought us to the brink of nuclear war, ecological self-destruction, political polarization, and civil war, and to the schizophrenic separation of cognition from the emotional subsoil which ought to nurture it.

Let us even go so far as to grant that, in the name of human dignity, the time for resistance is here, that obstruction and opposition are valid not only psychologically, for purposes of self-definition and independence, but also as the only recourse left to sensitive and reasonable men. There was a time when sane men ought to have assassinated Hitler and destroyed the Nazi machine; such a time is upon us again, one says, albeit in insidious and seductive guise. Let us grant even this.

And so it is time to join with Savio, who told us to "put our bodies on the machine and stop it." No more soggy incrementalism. No more seduction by co-opting institutions conducting paper tiger reforms which leave intact a fragmented consciousness and dehumanizing patterns of organization. No more talk of our "paranoia"—who isn't paranoid, when confronted with the terrifying list of realities we have been confronted with since our formative years? Let's welcome the Great Refusal of the sensitive and the intelligent to sell their brainpower to the generals and the ad men and the politicians.

The soap operas grind out their inexorable anguish; young men die because of the fears of the old; the toothpaste commercials, in their portrayals of relationships pivoting upon sex appeal, tell us what we are; the legislatures slumber; the computers hum, but all the data are not in yet, so we must be "deliberate" and "circumspect." To all this, you say, we must cry "Stop!" Do not tell us of our adolescence and our insanity, our identity diffusion and our hostilities, while we continue to be killed and our future consumed by the deadening roles we are asked to play. We admit that we cry out in anguish, the victims of insanity, but let us point the accusing finger in the right direction!

To all this, then, let us agree. But if we do, let us understand the implications fully: we *are victims.* As such, we bear the stamp of the distorted world which has spawned us. Our integrative energies, our passions and loyalties, lacking positive magnets, are drawn into opposition.

But can one make a truly meaningful life out of opposition alone? Do real communities grow in negation? To participate in the Great Refusal is only to silhouette real commitment; we are pale shadows of eros, and we substitute passionate rejection for passionate commitment and communion. It is a meager diet.

And it is especially undernourishing for the young. How tragic it is that the identity of a tender young person should first be fused in anguish rather than in joy! The time for resistance may be here, yes. But have we forgotten how to dream that our children will someday grow in the sunshine and not underground?

It's pathetic, really, how we try to plant the few healthy seeds of love and strength we have in the thin and shifting soil we occupy on the margins of the societal field. It's sad to hear a young man say that his first sense of real community came on the steps of the Pentagon, amidst clubs and blood; sadder still to see those who have learned to love the violence and the venom which alone seem to be capable of triggering communion for them. Sad to appraise the pathetic little collection of rootless symbols, like songs, guitars, rhetoric, flowers, and decals, which have been grafted onto marches and rallies—poor tokens of a life which should contain something stronger and richer and more central.

If only there were strong men in America, we wouldn't have it all backwards: opposition, dissent, even violence, are properly the tools of grown men who know from other, more positive experiences and sources, on behalf of what affirmations to use those tools. Men with positive identities should be using the tools of opposition today; then the young would not have to come of age and define themselves by acts of opposition alone.

But that is the price we pay; it was the price of the prophets, who robbed themselves of happiness because they could neither re-enter the society whose godlessness they saw, nor retreat to mountaintops to lick their wounds:

> And if I say, I shall not speak of Him, nor mention His name anymore, then there is in my heart a fire, burning deep into my bones; I weary myself to hold it in, but cannot.

Jeremiah was resigned to personal defeat because he loved too well the people he had to condemn; scorn and glibness were not parts of his repertoire; his anguish was that he could not protect himself with flight or callousness. And that is perhaps because he was filled not only with a critique of the then-existing current, but with a love for an Alternative as well. And in the end he left an impact on Western consciousness which no subsequent revolution has overturned.

That impact lies in the principle that protest is viable only when it involves affirmation. But one has to be very serious about what he affirms that transcends the society he denies; he cannot be sloppy about it. He must make his faith-assumptions bare. And live them. Otherwise he is the pitiable victim of the society he opposes. And that is where too many American "radicals" are at. They are stylistic radicals—uncritical, and sloppy about their alternatives. "Getting it together," alas, is basically a bad joke as a vision of what is to come after the revolution. One has to have more of a myth than that. And a few cultural vehicles to implement the myth.

In one such myth, God says to Abraham:

> Get yourself up, from out of your land, and from your roots and kindred, and from your father's house, unto the place that I will show you.

The radical break is there—as far-reaching as you can get. But the important part is the destination, or rather that there *is* one. For the passage continues "And I will make of you a nation, and I will bless you and make your name great." And then much more—quite ambitious. The text is thousands of years old; but somehow we are going to have to come to terms with the outrageous fact that it's happening largely in that way. In the survival of the Jew lies the crystallization of a radical message that alone has outlasted empires. It says that even more radical than "turning on" is the attempt to respond to a statement like "You shall be holy." It suggests that more radical than communism are the implications of the claim "The land is Mine."

I fear that we've all had such bad experiences with the prostitution of organized spirituality to the status quo that we are suspicious of this kind of talk. But we are hearing more and more about the spiritual these days—about the spiritual in its most demanding and consuming form. No matter what you say about it, you just aren't going to be able to do without it. Tillich suggests that when all of man's connections are horizontal—that is political, within history, and to other men—he is cut off from the only sources of human life which will permit him to face reality without despair. We have to reintroduce the vertical. But it can't be done just because we "need" it to inform our radicalism or to give cohesion to our pet projects; Hitler tried that. The vertical is more demanding; we have to meet it halfway. The spiritual cannot be enlisted for a cause, or introduced as an expedient, without becoming demonic.

In 1937, with storm clouds on the German horizon, Martin Buber offered what I think might become for me the most succinct spiritual critique of the atmosphere that is beginning to cloud our own radical sky:

> A certain impersonality occupies the space between man and man, begetting a strange distrust even in kindred spirits, an attitude of assumed superiority in critical appraisal of one's fellow. The other [becomes] a sum of qualities which are more or less useful to me. . . . Nothing is changed if the cause in regard to which I weighed his usability is a common cause. Impersonal analysis of a comrade makes barren the soil on which the community is based. Real faith . . . means holding ourselves open to the unconditional mystery which we encounter in every sphere of our life, and which cannot be comprised in any formula. At times it is difficult to live with the mystery . . . but there is the living transmission of those who have really lived with it, who are of our kind and who had our tidings. They help us through the pure strength with which they experienced the mystery, faced it, and engaged their lives to it. For to believe means to engage oneself. . . . We too can hear the voice ring forth from the black letters.[1]

The point, I hope, is clear: radicalism which gives a wide margin of credibility to spirituality, and spiritual traditions which transcend ahistorical impulse, have the chance to affirm and to succeed, to reach beyond the quagmire of the present. America's tragedy is that the vertical axes of mystery and faith have evaporated from her cultural and political consciousness. Are her radicals, in their fist-clenching and teeth-gnashing, to become the most tragic casualties of all?

NOTES

1. Martin Buber, *Israel and the World*, New York: Schocken Books, pp. 49–50.

American Jews react to the existence of the State of Israel in many ways. Born in a period of unprecedented tragedy and triumph in the struggle for the Jewish people's liberation, hailed in the forties by progressive and revolutionary elements the world over, the state exercises a compelling attraction for some young Americans, exacerbates problems of Jewish identity for others. The four essays which follow suggest that young Jews must unapologetically confront both the moral and personal implications of their inevitable involvement with the fate of Israel. The essays' honesty and lack of equivocation, even when critical of the third Palestinian Jewish commonwealth in history, make refreshing reading.

The first piece was written by Gabriel Ende, who was a graduate student in history and education at the University of Chicago a year before he emigrated to Israel. He does not make a plea for living in Israel, but rather deals with his own personal response to the difficulties and discomforts of the American Jewish radical who cannot divorce his Jewish identity from his social commitment. A great number of young Jews struggle with this tension; not all resolve the problem in favor of aliyah (moving to Israel), but most accept it as an active and intriguing possibility. What makes Gabe Ende's remarks seem very authentic is their grounding in experience and struggle rather than in stale ideology and oblivious rhetoric.

Leaving All This Behind:
Reflections on
a Matured Zionist Commitment[*]

────────

by GABRIEL ENDE

Jewish publicists and spokesmen have made the word "assimilation" famous. It suffuses our journals like the freckles on the face of the all-American boy featured on television commercials. Everyone by now knows that "assimilation" is "bad." Even the American Jewish Committee, which for decades has paraded under the banner of "greater Jewish integration into American life," now vigorously proclaims that "integration does not mean assimilation." And so on.

This ever-increasing fear of assimilation is matched by a growing recognition of the inroads that have already been made among American Jews. Amidst the profusion of sociological studies, learned and unlearned articles, and anti-assimilationist theorizing can be heard the Zionist plea for *aliyah*. "Go to Israel," it insists, "and this won't happen to your children. Besides, you'll lead a more complete Jewish life." This may sound fair enough (or sim-

[*] This selection originally appeared in *Response*, Vol. III, No. 2, Fall 1969.

plistically unfair), but it does not address itself to the situation of the socially conscious and committed Jew, who is temporarily preoccupied with finding *his own* role, and meeting the needs of *his own* condition. Assimilation is not his *personal* fear, nor is it a primary source of moral, social or political challenge to him. But "assimilation" does not bespeak the totality of disabilities which are inherent in the American *galut* (exile). There are other, far more personal ones, which abrade upon the psyche and threaten the very integrity of modern men. Whether the individual cares to notice their presence, they touch very deeply upon his above-mentioned problems of *role* and *condition*. And, as problems of *galut,* they admit of a "Zionist" response.

If American Jews have popularized the notion of "assimilation," the Blacks have done the same for the concept of "manhood." "You have robbed us of our manhood," they tell us, "and we must now regain it." No one would question that claim, yet how many people really know what "lack of manhood" really means? It certainly does not refer to one's inability to walk down the street and feel "I am a man," as some pathetically obtuse "Concerned White" once explained to me. Yet if we Jews take an intelligent look into our own experience, we can discover the meaning of this condition. It has a lot to do with the Russian Haskalah dictum of "Be a Jew in your house and a *man* outside it." It has to do with the way that Jewish causes are argued in the presence of non-Jews. It has to do with the language that one speaks, the symbols and images that one invokes, the "traditional" expressions that one uses to color one's language, the categories of analysis into which everything must be placed, and the very values which one seeks to impress upon others. In essence, "lack of manhood" refers to a condition in which a person is abnormally inhibited in his self-expression or self-assertion. The black man who cannot assert his right to provide for his family or to publicly voice his views on an issue is suffering from a malady whose Jewish variant is perhaps best reflected in the differences between what we say among committed Jews and among non-Jews (not to mention non-committed Jews). How we have to watch our words in the latter's presence! How we have to tailor our speech to the demands of the particular milieu in which we find ourselves! How much concealment, pandering, moral and semantic juggling are involved in the process! A specifically Jewish concern is not regarded as legitimate in and of itself, but must be validated by reference to an external American and/or transcendent moral concern. And the poor Jew who is arguing the cause (or has found some convenient reason for not arguing it), is this pathetic creature really a "man"?

But the problem is far more pervasive. Express yourself in Jewish frames of reference on an issue (never mind the language) and you'll be utterly incomprehensible to your peers. Teach the Russian Revolution to a high school class composed mainly of Jews (as I have), and try to develop an appreciation of the significant Jewish role without having to sneak it through the back door, and without eliciting an embarrassed reaction on the part of most of the Jewish students. Join a general organization of any sort and try to react to issues as a *Jew* without soon developing the feeling of being a *kvetch*. Note the tragi-comic communal reaction of hysteria to Philip Roth's novels, however open they may be to enlightened criticism. Judaism is clearly not a matter of public domain in the United States.

The problem of "manhood" is closely linked to that of "integrity." Above all, modern man demands personal integration. He will not tolerate the maintenance of contradictory values or beliefs, nor will he blandly suppress one part of his being to enjoy another part of it. But we American Jews do that every day. One cannot blame the decline of Jewish observance primarily upon the demands of the non-Jewish world; yet every honest Jew knows that to

some extent this is the case. *Shabbat,* for example, inter-
feres with complete social involvement, as does *kashrut.*
Now few people will question the need of tradition to reconcile itself with the demands of important social activity
(such as an anti-war march on the *Shabbat* or the prospect
of spending a summer with a family in a poverty area),
but we must realize that many of these conflicts would not
occur were we living in a predominantly Jewish society.
What is a Jewish teacher in a city school to do when he
finds that Jewish holidays account for seven of the first
twenty days he is to spend in the classroom? Something
within him declares that the crystallization of these conflicts—his need to decide between the "Jewish" and the
"human" components in his being (or the desperate response which allows for performing the activity as a *mitzvah*)—isn't fair. But it is fair, much more fair than the
demand that American society restructure itself to meet
Jewish needs for integrity and manhood.

The anti-Jewish backlash of the New Left has recently
put another aspect of the American Jew's condition into
broad relief. Whenever we associate ourselves with a
cause, we cannot do so "nakedly"; we always have to carry
with us a peripheral concern—often a reservation—based
on how the realization of that cause (which we can't control) will affect basic Jewish needs. How many times have
committed Jews joined with others in Vietnam and student power rallies, only to have their erstwhile compan-
ions stab them in the back with boorish anti-Israel remarks on the morrow? "All power to the people," but must
I passively accept a situation in which no black militant
dares publicly to challenge the increasingly fashionable
anti-Semitic rhetoric of the movement? How should I feel;
where should I turn? Should I piously lecture myself
about the dishonor of injecting Jewish reservations into
causes as important as these? Should I browbeat myself
into believing that all the dangers are imaginary?

For some reason, the whole situation reminds me of

the fatuous reasoning of the Jewish Narodniks. The Narodniks were members of a student-led, socialist-oriented, Russian populist movement of the late nineteenth century. As the imminence of the pogroms of 1881 became apparent, the movement, after some deliberation, decided to participate in them in view of its overriding interest in arousing the masses. The numerous Jews in the movement, after some additional hesitation, decided to join in as well, on the desperate theory that only their affluent, exploitative co-religionists would be attacked. But that, of course, was not the case. . . .

I am also plagued by the recollection of the fearful loneliness that I experienced as I sat in a dormitory room with four non-Jews, watching the televised aftermath of Robert Kennedy's assassination. They may not have been aware of what was on my mind, but I was all too aware of the eventual revulsion with "Jewish political demands" which would come to some of theirs. Once again, the integration is lacking. To hedge in one's commitment to a general cause is shameful, but not to hedge is foolish and sometimes ethnically treacherous.

The Jew is not the only victim of his situation, however. Judaism has suffered just as much. Cultures develop as people respond to challenges that are posed to them. These challenges may run a very wide gamut, from military threats and scarcity of water to the lures of foreign life-styles, and demands for solutions to burning social issues. In the process of responding to these challenges, cultures become temporarily disorganized, and strongly held values give way to uncertainty. But in the long run, the cultures are refined, enriched, and made more relevant. And although such changes are difficult to discern overnight, few observers remain unaware of the strong injection that involvement in the civil rights and peace movements has given Christianity. At a time when organized religion is declining, Jesus has once again been resurrected into a hero.

Now this did not have to happen. Were the respective movements to have shunned overtly Christian values, symbols, expressions, traditions, heroes, ceremonials, and organizational affiliations in the course of their efforts, the above effect would not have been produced. But America is fundamentally a Christian society, with its clergy seeking causes with which to revitalize their religion. So it was not merely expedient but also natural for a good part of these struggles to assume a Christian frame of reference. Hence, in the minds of much of its membership, Christianity is intimately linked to the principles of brotherhood and peace. Given the skillful exploitation of these elements by its present and future leaders, the church's character will hereafter reflect this attitude.

One can point as well to the efforts of Jews to co-opt these causes, but the very terminology betokens the futility of these efforts. When all is said and done, all that we have tried to do is jump on the "religio-social-action" bandwagon. Those committed Jews who involved themselves in these issues at an early stage did not bring a Jewish focus to them. It would have been unnatural to do so. When, for instance, the Queens College SDS held a sit-in at an induction center several years ago, they chose to sing Christmas carols to dramatize their activity, although the chairman and almost all of the members were Jewish. The American people cannot be aroused by the invocation of Jewish symbols or models. One certainly cannot appeal (except superficially) to this country's oppressed minorities in that fashion. Nor can you even appeal to many committed Jews, for they know—despite all the cumbersome apologetics to the contrary—that the problems were fostered in a non-Jewish environment and will have to be resolved in that same environment in terms appropriate to it. *All that the public use of a Jewish perspective can accomplish is to isolate the Jewish activists from the mainstream of the movement.* This may be viewed as good for us, but in terms of the cause as a whole, it is at best (ex-

cept where Jewish interests are particularly and sepa-
rately involved) a put-on.

So Judaism itself suffers from *galut*. Of course, there
are times when its nature is somewhat affected by changes
occurring in neighboring cultures (witness the partial
elaboration of a Social Gospel ethic—as opposed to mere
charity—on the heels of its development by the Protes-
tants in the late nineteenth century), and there is some
feedback even when our aping of the *goyim* is as crude as
it is now. But the lack of genuineness in the absortive
process is reflected in the murkiness of the eventual assimilation. Contrast this, however, with the radical effect that
the kibbutz movement, *kibbutz galuyot* (the ingathering
of exiles), and the Israel Defense Forces have had upon
Israeli Judaism, and even upon many committed American Jews. Their imprints will never be erased. This is because the Jewish context is the most natural one—if not
the only one—in which the goals of these and similar
movements could be realized. Hence, every challenge in
Israel is potentially a *liberating* and enriching one for Judaism, and not a source of fear (assimilatory or otherwise)
and self-enclosement, as is all too often the case in
America.

A plea for *aliyah* will not follow here, although one is
certainly in order. There is much pioneering work to be
done in the American Jewish community, not the least of
which is the development of approaches to meet the above-
mentioned problems. Still, one would hope that any such
efforts will be free of the oft-accompanying illusion of the
non-exilic nature of our situation in the United States.
America, however well we've been treated here, is clearly
galut and as an increasing number of sensitive young Jews
realize the extent to which their would-be "integrated
Jewish personalities" are being violated here, they will
seriously consider the option of life in Israel. And they will
be able, in my opinion, to achieve far greater fulfillment
than those who remain behind in America.

James Sleeper spent a month in Israel learning about Arab-Jewish relations projects, speaking with Jews and Israeli Arabs in an effort to assess the potential for rapprochement of any kind between two warring peoples in their shared homeland. Skeptical of both radical student pronouncements against Israel, and of certain Zionist perspectives, he addresses his findings to American students who experience some of the confusion and skepticism which motivated his own visit.

Israeli Arabs:
Israel's Peaceful Frontier?

———

by JAMES A. SLEEPER

American Jews, especially those on campuses, have long been exposed to the claim that the State of Israel is at best a mixed blessing. We have had to grant a measure of truth to the argument that the creation of the state caused human suffering as well as alleviating it; that in this century a powerful Jewish myth came alive along with an equally powerful movement for Arab renaissance and liberation from colonial abuse. We have learned, in fact, that to view the state Jewishly ought to mean that we submit it to a severe critique, that we accept the crystallization of the Jewish people and the Jewish historical message into a political state as, at best, problematic.

But are we to accept as well the stereotypes which portray Israel as an "outpost of Western imperialism," as a haven for "Arab-hating aggressors"? Are we to believe the world's goodwill can replace armed force as a guarantor of the minimal physical survival of peoples? Are we to be

apologetic about the Jewish experiment in Palestine, to ignore the fact that this is not the first but at least the third
Jewish commonwealth to exist there, to dismiss as unen-
lightened and parochial Israel's enrichment of the notion
of particularism in a world gone mad on "universalism"?
Clearly, if we are talking about a critique which is severe,
we must be just as hard on these stereotypes as we ought
to be on American Jewry's glib celebration of Jewish statehood.

With both the traditional Hebrew school myths and
the anti-Israel stereotypes in mind, I went to Israel to see
for myself. It seemed to me that one acid test of the validity of the charges that Israel is exploitive and anti-Arab
might be sought among the three hundred thousand Arabs
who have been granted a sort of second-class citizenship
there for the past twenty years. The lot of these Arabs had
better be confronted before conclusions are reached about
the mentality of their Jewish "oppressors." And the "oppressors" ought to be confronted, too. With this challenge,
I embarked upon what admittedly could be nothing more
than a microcosmic, person-to-person venture—a probing
of attitudes, and not an exhaustive political analysis or an
attempt to gather statistics. What do the Jews think of
their "enemies"? Are both peoples willing to share their
homeland?

My basic assumption was that to answer these questions ideological charges and stereotypes had to be set
aside to make room for what may be really fruitful criticisms of Israel—criticisms that might justly be made by
those whose concerns are for the meaning of Jewishness
and for basic human rights.

But ideological charges and stereotypes die hard, even
when they are held by individuals whose actual concern
and information about Arabs and Jews is at best minimal.
First, then, I would like to explore the anti-Israel stereotypes' meanings to some of the American students who
embrace them. Then I will describe what I saw in Israel,

and, lastly, I will try to indicate what kind of American student action outside of glib pronouncements can best nurture the few small seeds of hope I found planted.

The Stereotype's Appeal— and Its Limitations

Although Arab territorial nationalism, like Zionism, is a twentieth-century phenomenon ("We both woke up at the same time," says one Jewish author), it is assumed in the popular anti-Israel position that Arabs, like the blacks of Africa, are indigenous and rightful rulers in Palestine. Personally I think this flouting of historical evidence is open to some question: the Jewish people's unusual history has scarcely been characterized by nationalism, let alone "imperialism," since the end of the last Jewish commonwealth in Palestine, which fell to the Romans in 70 A.D. Americans should know that the Palestinian Jew regards himself as a freedom fighter who owes the world precious little after years of exile and persecution; he sees himself as a member of the third, if not the "fourth" (i.e., the Jewish) world.

Nevertheless, the stereotype persists, not because it serves very well to clarify the causality and complexity of Palestinian Jewish nationhood in our own times, but because:

1) It corresponds rather neatly to the perspective of Frantz Fanon, a well-known African writer and spokesman for the liberation of colonized peoples, who is justifiably popular with many students. A link is made between his powerful portrayal of heroic freedom fighters, like the African and Asian guerillas, and the *El Fatah*. That the Jewish soldier, in lashing out against the Arabs, stepping on the toes of the great powers, and thumbing his nose at centuries of Western inquisition, also feels himself a freedom fighter in his ancestors' land is not given credibility.

2) The stereotype has something in common with

the facts of America's treatment of blacks and Indians,
two agonizing problems in the face of which few of us
escape a feeling of helplessness. If Arabs in Israel are second-class citizens we can indict the Israelis for some of the
crimes we ourselves would like to atone for—this time,
however, by "solving" a problem that seems manageable
and soluble from a distance of twelve thousand miles.

3) Israel appears to be so much the creation of students' middle-class Jewish parents. It seems to be the
summer haven of Portnoy's people and of the American
Jewish community, a group well known to students for
having subordinated whatever was good and radical in Judaism to the norms and aesthetics of middle-class culture.
How such wealthy Americans are actually regarded by Israelis might be of interest to American students who think
they know what sarcasm is. The situation and style of life
in Israel is not the creation of those who gave money to
Israel; they made possible, but did not shape—and often
might not even approve of—all of the country's development.

In thus questioning the accuracy or emotional relevance of the stereotype, I am not attempting to dismiss
criticisms of Israel. In fact, it was under the suspicion that
the stereotype might be partly true that I went to Israel to
learn about the Movement for Arab-Jewish Cooperation—
a small, non-utopian group whose name belies its tiny size.
I went not only with the criticisms of American students
in mind, however, but also with the suspicion that ultimately Israel should not be opposed or justified by the
substitution of one ideology for another, be it Fanonism
for Zionism, or vice versa. We cannot really pretend to be
softening the prejudices of the belligerents (assuming that
is a goal) until we have determined to stop feeding our
own.

The attempt to disregard these conflicting caricatures
(but not historical perspective) became relatively simple
after my arrival; all claims appear rather pale and con-

torted in the face of complex and fascinating reality.

A Jewish doctor who, during the Six Day War, traveled about the countryside visiting and reassuring frightened Arab friends said, "You may travel the length and breadth of our land, but you will not find hatred of Arabs." Alas, his statement was not true; when I told a class at Bar Ilan University of the doctor's wartime visits, they thought him suspect or at best demented. On the whole, however, when we speak of Israelis' feelings toward Arabs, we are *not* talking about the kind of teeth-gnashing hatred that some of us thought we saw on television reports from Cairo in June of 1967. We who criticize Israel are not trying to restrain imperialism as much as to calm a fertile paranoia and at the same time to respect a mighty determination not to become another sad episode in the history of Jewish persecution. We shall return to this paranoia and determination, for it is difficult for many who are outside the stream of Jewish history to understand the difference between fear and hate in national character. For now, suffice it to say that in attacking so-called "imperialism," some American students have failed to see what *is* potentially wrong with Israel, and therefore lose their opportunity to solve the problem of Israeli overreaction and indifference to Arab suffering. But perhaps solving such delicate problems is not on the agenda for ideologues and Jewish self-haters; it is hard enough for even the open-minded to calm a Jewish soldier who says, "If we were not to oppress anyone here, they would still be slaughtering us in the diaspora"—a statement which is admittedly difficult to disprove, unless one is hopelessly naive about Jewish history.

It is one thing, too, to advocate a guerilla war against a government which oppresses its people, and which is not representative of the populace it controls. It is quite another thing to oppose a nation in which the population, to a man, will rise in defense of any attack, real or imagined. The state of Israel certainly enjoys a solidarity of support from its Jewish inhabitants; and during the Six Day War, even the three hundred thousand Israeli Arabs were quiet and often courageously loyal—which may be explained, of course, in a variety of ways. As far as the Jewish inhabitants of Israel are concerned, anyway, the fact of the state's existence—unlike that of the Thieu-Ky government—cannot be wished away, or even conquered away, unless, of course, one has in the back of his mind another attempt at genocide. As far as the Arab inhabitants are concerned, I asked them to explain for themselves their cooperation during the war.

Israeli Arabs Facing Israel's Existence

The first realization impressed upon me in my discussions with Arabs is that Israel's existence is something that many of her Arab citizens have had to come to terms with on more than an *ad hoc* basis. In fact, one Arab teacher and journalist said to me, "I could speak to you in English, but I want to have you practice your Hebrew so that you may come and live here." What was he driving at?

The answer may be found in the words of another young Arab, who works in a government tax office in Haifa. His is one of the few Arab families who failed to respond to the demands of Trans-Jordan and Syria that they leave Israel in 1948 and return on the heels of victorious Arab armies, but who chose instead to heed the pleas of Israelis that they remain and accept citizenship. He said, "When you've lived among Jews, you know that they are not monsters, that they too have a right to be here, and that we might as well learn to live together." The more Jews who agree, the better off he is; hence the encouragement from Israeli Arabs for the immigration of sympathetic American students to Israel.

When I asked another Arab teacher, who had been fired after bureaucratic harassment and reinstated through the efforts of Jewish friends, what kind of model he presents to his Arab students as a way of relating to Israelis, he said, "First, I want to correct your wording; we are Israelis, too. Our fate is inseparable from that of Israel." It is not easy for a young Arab to establish his identity as an Israeli in a nation whose heroes are Moshe Dayan and the paratroopers. Yet young Arab teachers struggle to make their students aware of their stake in Israel.

Why? I doubt that their attitude is that of a few Uncle Toms; they are hardly rewarded for such conciliatory views. An Arab who speaks up as they do for full rights *as Israeli citizens* is scrutinized by the Israeli Security Police as a possible agitator, and at the same time threatened by Arab guerillas as a "collaborator" with the Israelis.

In private, at least, the same individuals who try to be good Israelis will not hesitate to cite abuses and harassments by members of the Israel government and police, spurred on by a frightened Jewish populace. Yet despite the often arbitrary restrictions which have at times been imposed upon them, these vocal Arabs keep working for rapprochement because they realize that Israeli Arabs are 1) religiously and culturally free, 2) materially better off than elsewhere, and 3) now being provided with the educational tools to help overcome psychological and other disadvantages.*

I saw these facts myself, and I suspect that being treated as a human being goes hand in hand with cultural liberation. These Arabs claim that in the event of a conquest of Israel they would be jailed along with the Jews, if not in fact treated more harshly; at any rate, in such a situation, there would be acts of resistance and courage by these Arabs which would not be explainable in current American student ideology.

Of course one major setback to material and educational

---

* These are generalizations; the schools which Arabs are required to attend under compulsory, tax-supported education, emphasize Jewish over Arab culture. But a recent issue of the Hebrew University student paper sought to emphasize that the number of Arabs enrolled there is increasing significantly. It is a patchwork quilt, but the basic principles are clear.

progress came in the political reorientation in the wake of
the Six Day War, which led to the incorporation of new
Arab populations and the subsequent terrorism. Every
Arab was suspect again. When a bomb blew up in the Tel
Aviv railroad station, angered Jews attacked innocent
Arab bystanders. Despite the fact that many such Jewish
assailants are now in jail, and that soldiers went from
house to house in the neighborhood of the station caution-
ing young people against a recurrence of such arbitrary
retaliation, this kind of incident is immeasurably harmful
in its contribution to the escalation of mistrust.

Even more serious was the bombing of the Hebrew
University cafeteria. There are only five hundred Arab
students at Israel's four universities but the number had
been growing, and Arabs with university degress were beginning to have great influence in changing the lot of their
people in Israel. Needless to say, this kind of success is
threatening to Arab guerillas who need the support of
Arab populations in Israel, and the explosion in the University may have the effect of slowing educational progress for Israeli Arabs.

Israeli Jews Facing Israeli Arabs

Even without terrorist incidents, however, most of the
work of rapprochement must be done among the Jews
themselves, and the reasons are not surprising:

1)   A large part of Israel's population is composed of
refugees or the children of refugees from Hitler's Europe
—refugees, as one of them put it bitterly, "for whom there
were no United Nations commissions and no sympathetic
American students." The concern of these people is hardly
with the Arabs as much as with the reestablishment of a
life without fear for themselves. Of course there are beautiful exceptions; world famous Yichiel Di-Nur, author of
House of Dolls, who writes eloquently and works dili-
gently on behalf of Arab-Jewish reconciliation, bears in-

delibly upon his arm the record of other men's plans for
him. It would be easy to understand indifference to Arabs
in the midst of an attempt to repair a shattered existence,
and, despite Mr. Di-Nur and others like them, this indifference is to be found.

2) There are in Israel today five hundred thousand
Jewish refugees from Arab lands—Jews who fled mob violence which erupted in those countries upon the establishment of Israel's or their own independence, and in the
wake of the Six Day War. More technologically backward
than their fellow European Jews, these immigrants to Israel have some reason to resent their Arab backgrounds—
and Arabs who remind them of their past.

3) There is in Israel the struggle for a convincing
model of Jewish masculinity, denied the Jew for two thousand years. Liberation of the downtrodden involves, according to writers like Fanon, the kind of violent self-
assertion which the young North African Jew manifests in
the Israeli army, in a manner reminiscent of the deeds of
valor of American blacks in the Second World War. Such
soldiers are not likely to return home from the front to
work in the subtle and torturous vineyard of Arab-Jewish
relations; it takes a more sophisticated notion of maturity
to encompass that kind of endeavor, and while Israel probably does at least as good a job as the United States of
disassociating violence from masculinity, we can understand the difficulty with which this is achieved: "The
world does not understand what it is to make war while
being ashamed of fighting," says one soldier; "Excuse us,
we've won." Is the fighting Jew being dehumanized by
war? That is an unusual concern for a country battling for
its existence; yet, as many articles and discussions I saw
suggest, it is not far from the minds of many Israelis.

4) The very Orthodox religious Jews in Israel constitute a segment of the population which, despite its mistrust of the secular Israeli state, holds no love for infidel
Arabs. The religious impulse for justice is thus blunted by

the fact that religious perspectives are usually the monopoly of leaders who cannot reach beyond their parochial interests to embrace human need.

5) The atmosphere of warmaking is present even if subdued and protracted. Young Americans simply do not know what it is to be totally at one with a society at war. We do not even know what it is to be at one with our country in time of peace. I am not saying that our Israeli counterparts are rabid nationalists who experience no twinges of alienation from any aspects of their society. In fact the satire and intellectual freedom in Israel make it clear that there is dissatisfaction. In a Tel Aviv cabaret I watched Israeli entertainers mock the army and proclaim, to a catchy tune, "I'm not interested in fulfilling promises that God made to Abraham"—a direct repudiation of the "full Israel" supposedly promised the patriarch by God, and which is often cited as Scriptural proof that Israelis are expansionists. All this despite the fact that daily incidents of terrorism create the kind of tension that ought to breed mob unity and silence debate. When that tension does lead to anti-Arab feeling, it's not surprising.

To be sure, if one travels the length and breadth of Israel he can find hatred of Arabs, for all the above reasons. I met that hatred in a remark on a bus, in a class at Bar Ilan University, in a conversation with a friend. But one learns to combat hatred not because it is unexplainable or even senseless, but minimally because, in the long run, it is inhuman and self-defeating.

Israeli Jews themselves deserve some credit for the good that is being done. It might be easier for a Southern American white to champion civil rights for blacks than for an Israeli Jew to lead a crusade for Arab citizens—after all, there is a war going on; our own treatment of American German and Japanese citizens during World Wars I and II may serve to clarify this point.

Yet, "amidst the rising tide of hate, blood, and misery . . . loom the nightmarish memories of the Jewish holocaust. With the scars of memory still fresh in their minds, Nina and Yichiel Di-Nur opened their home so that Jews and Arabs might have a place to meet and through personal contact achieve greater human understanding." So began the brief history of the Movement for Arab-Jewish Cooperation, the organization which facilitated my visit to Israel. Through several early movement projects hundreds of Jewish and Arab Israelis were in fact brought together. Keynoting the movement's efforts was the late Prime Minister Eshkol's statement on cooperation between Jews and Arabs.

> This cannot be the work of government clerks. . . . The matter must be tackled on a tremendously broad front. In effect the total population has an obligation to involve itself in this effort.

In Israel I traveled with Mrs. Di-Nur to meet Arabs and to view projects now underway. Butrus Dahli, an Arab graduate of the Hebrew University who returned from Jerusalem to his native village, has sponsored exchange visits between students in Kfar Yasif and Jewish kibbutz youth, and he dreams of an exchange center as a facility dedicated to this kind of activity.

At the University of Haifa, I witnessed an exciting and fruitful meeting of Arab and Jewish students. "Why don't you open your mouths?" a Jewish student just back from reserve duty challenged the Arabs present. "We want to know what you mean when you say that your fate is inseparable from that of the Jewish state."

"We are afraid to explain what that means," responded an Arab boy.

"We musn't be," declared an Arab high school teacher, who proceeded to recount his own experiences in speaking frankly with mistrustful Jews. A small enough beginning, but the feeling in the room at the close of the meeting was indescribable.

In Nahariya, near Acre, I attended one of a series of evening meetings between Arab and Jewish adults. What on the surface might have seemed like a weekly book club meeting in a suburban American home was actually an important exchange between members of two ancient peoples in their shared homeland. The guest was a British newspaperwoman who reported her experiences in refugee camps for Arabs in Gaza and the West Bank.

In Ashkelon, I met Shirley and Shlomo Shpira, who have been trying, despite insurmountable red tape, to open a vocational school in Gaza for Arab children. In Jerusalem, Dr. Jack Cohen of Hillel told me of painstaking and frustrating efforts to establish trust and communication among Arab and Jewish students, and of attempts to enable some of the students to work in VISTA fashion in Arab villages this summer.

I had no monopoly on information about groups and projects; most of these I found largely by word of mouth, and so it may be assumed that the efforts I discovered are representative of a larger number of undertakings and common sentiments throughout the country.

Toward a Realistic Approach

I keep remembering the words of one of the Jewish members of the Nahariya evening discussion group: "Israel is special, and therefore we are being judged severely. We are being asked to act as giants. Yes, there is hostility toward Arabs. But no other people would have done as well as we are doing." As much as this statement smacks of apologetics, and as little as it contributes to the solution of the problems that still exist, it is a difficult claim to refute, and part of a necessary corrective on ideological blindness.

There are true stories of arbitrary jailings and beatings of Arabs suspected by the government of terrorism, and there is certainly some of the same kind of prejudice and partisan law enforcement which characterizes the United States; the danger that nationalism may gather momentum to the exclusion of other values exists. But moral self-consciousness exists as well, and Americans should know that that is a rare enough quality.

Things have not improved much since my visit; with each continuing month of impasse, divisions widen. But it is my impression that tender seeds of peace and accomodation have begun to grow; they must be nurtured, because both peoples have a claim to the land, and because the supposed purging, ennobling effects of violence do not exist in such a moral standoff.

While my observations have assumed as given the existence of a Jewish state, they should not be interpreted as a blanket defense of statehood. Self-denial on the chauvinistic level may be a part of what Judaism is all about. Certainly since the time of Samuel, who cautioned the people against crowning a king and becoming "like all the nations," we Jews have struggled uncomfortably with the territorial, political level of self-definition; we have learned from our history that our power to move heaven and earth has had little to do with armies and states. This is not a critique based on ignorance or self-hatred, but upon a serious reading of our history and of the paradigms in our tradition.

One does not question the fact that physical survival is a prerequisite to other considerations. In the wake of the Holocaust and the massive indifference of the rest of the world to the plight of the Jews, the struggle for liberation of 1948 was necessary and justified, as well as instinctive. But there is nothing about such a reflex response which automatically makes all its consequences morally desirable or tactically wise; the fact is that we pay an enormous price and face enormous dangers in remaining inflexible. That is sad because there is nothing inherently "reactionary" or "oppressive" about the Jewish community of Palestine; one would have to be ideologically blinded not to see its incredible soul and potential. The responsibility of American Jews who travel to Israel is to carry with them both the vision and the critique. The seductive balm of personal wholeness and "at-homeness" in one's land must not be allowed to stifle the universalism and criticism of the prophets, who also lived in the land, at once in love with and estranged from their people.

The challenge to young Americans—and to young Arabs studying in America—is firstly to visit Israel and see for themselves. I was allowed to move freely without credentials or introductions, and was impressed not only by the degree of intellectual and political freedom, but also by the accessibility of members of the government and intelligentsia to one who was introduced simply as "an American student." But more importantly, I was impressed with the need for Americans and Israelis to keep testing and enlarging that freedom, and with the need for us to confront Israelis with the claims I have been discussing, and to bring to bear upon Israeli representatives in this country the pressure of informed, moral opinion.

On our campuses we should not be afraid of abandoning the simplistic stereotypes of some fellow students who are glibly "anti-Israel," and the stereotypes, on the other hand, of uninformed segments of the Jewish community who embrace a "cowboy and Indian" view of the Israeli-Arab conflict. We ought to read *New Outlook* and publications of the nascent Israeli new left, as well as American magazines like *Liberation*—all of which are increasingly available in university newsstands and bookstores. We ought to sponsor meetings with both Palestinians and Israeli Arabs who come to America.

A generation of Americans which manifests unparalleled moral and human sensitivity is worthy of more than button-wearing and sloganeering when it comes to the Middle East. Those who have taken glib stands on the situation there must learn to respond to undramatic calls to plant a few seeds of peace and cooperation in ambiguous and shifting soil. They might, in the process, learn to affirm something about the difficult and sensitive and moral nature of peace-building in other areas of the world as well.

Michael J. Rosenberg is the antithesis of the Jewish apologist. His article "To Uncle Tom and Other Such Jews," which was published widely in newspapers and magazines on many campuses during 1968, created something of a sensation in the Jewish radical community. His essay about Israel in this volume, addressed not to Arab claims but to American students who oppose Israel, speaks powerfully for itself. A graduate of the State University of New York at Albany, where he majored in history, Michael is currently in the Department of Contemporary Jewish Studies at Brandeis. He has written for Midstream, the Village Voice, and the Jerusalem Post.

Israel without Apology

by MICHAEL J. ROSENBERG

The twenty-five years since V-E Day have seen so many changes for so many peoples. In 1945 Germany was a devastated nation. Occupied by the four allied powers, she seemed unlikely to rise again. Today Germany is the strong man of Europe. Her currency and her people far outpace those of Britain and France. Today the talk is about European unity, a United States of Europe. The old alliances have been reshuffled. The Second World War is very much in the past. Today's world is radically different.

And for the Jewish people the situation is apparently greatly changed. The crematoria are stilled. Six million of our people are dead. But the very success of that last European pogrom assure us that there will be no more. Not in Europe, anyway.

Zionist dream has been realized. There is today a Jewish State. She is viable. In fact Herzl's fantastic vision is, to an amazing degree, a reality.

Apparently the overall Jewish condition has changed dramatically. The very idea of the Jewish flag waving over Jerusalem can be viewed as proof of that change.

And yet nothing fundamental has changed. We are waging the same battle for survival that we have been fighting since the diaspora began. The rules that govern all other men in 1970 do not apply to us. We are still the pariah among nations. For two thousand years our unique and terrible situation could have been viewed as a product of our statelessness. We were told that the other nations were frightened at the sight of this ghostlike people who had no land. People are only hospitable to those who have their own home. We had none. Thus we frightened them and they hated us.

Today we see the truth. We have a state "like any other state." Ben-Gurion proudly pointed to Jewish prostitutes in a Jewish country spending time in Jewish prisons. Normalcy. But it isn't so. Israel is a nation unlike any other.

As a small new nation in Asia, populated by a dark Semitic people who threw off the yoke of Western imperialism in a protracted war of independence, Israel is an obvious candidate for membership in the Third World bloc. Her destiny must lie with the other new states of Asia and Africa. But the fact is that Israel is not a part of the Third World. The nations of that bloc, for the most part, oppose Israel and are more than a little skeptical of her right to exist. And moreover it is hard to classify Israel as one of the developing new nations. Israel, with a standard of living comparable to Western Europe's, with her high degree of industrialization and with her own technical aid programs to Asia, Africa and Latin America, is plainly not in the "developing" category. Even in a geographic sense Israel is an anomaly. An Asian nation by definition, her population is largely European as are her modern cultural, political and philosophical roots. But of course she is not a European nation. A new nation, she is one of the few on the planet inhabited today by the same people who did so two thousand years ago. Any Israeli youngster can with ease read manuscripts left by his ancestors thousands of years ago. And yet Israel is a new nation.

Politically Israel clearly would fit in with the Western bloc. Her main enemy is the Soviet Union. Her leaders are strongly anti-communist. She is democratic and she needs the United States. However, even in dealing with the United States, which has as the core of its foreign policy the program of unstinting assistance to each and every anti-communist government, Israel is treated as an outcast. As the President of the United States has pointed out, the United States is neither pro- nor anti-Israel.

It becomes clear that the Zionists were wrong. Israel can never be a "state like any other state." And the question arising out of the unending Middle East conflict is thus not whether there is room on this planet for a small independent state, but whether there is room for a small, independent *Jewish* State. No one questions the existence of any of the other small and relatively powerless nations that fill the United Nations. No one questions their right to a territory and a flag. We may be living in a post-nationalist era, but the fact is that all the post-national peoples have their states and their anthems.

Those who question the validity of the nation-state appear to do so when it is the Jewish State that is discussed. And that is why all the analogies are invalid. Israel is not Czechoslovakia, for Czechoslovakia is one of many Eastern European states. And Israel is not the tragic Biafra. For Biafra was one of many small African nations. And Israel has little in common with the Palestinian Arabs who can take comfort in the fact that there are thirteen Arab states, not one of which is threatened with any form of national calamity. But there is only one Jewish State, without allies, unique and ultimately alone. And that is why all the analogies are invalid. Israel is the Jewish State, the one Jewish State. And she is threatened with extinction.

And thus Israel is the ultimate reality in the life of every Jew living today. I believe that Israel surpasses in importance Jewish ritual. It is more than the Jewish tradition; and, in fact, it is more than the Mosaic law itself. The anti-religious Jew who supports Israel is welcomed as a Jew and as an integral part of the community. The observant Jew who does not accept the centrality of the modern state of Israel is not accepted and is rarely even tolerated. In dealing with those who oppose Israel, we are not reasonable and we are not rational. Nor should we be.

For Israel is linked in an inextricable and direct way with that most irrational of all tragedies, the Holocaust. Need it be repeated that six million Jews were murdered because they were Jews? Need anyone be reminded that the word "genocide," so loosely applied today, was created to describe the massacre of one third of the Jewish people? And Israel is the last refuge of the survivors of Hitler's final solution. In Israel you cannot escape the manifestations of this fact. Until recently the Israeli radio station featured a daily program called "Who Knows? Who Remembers?" on which descriptions were given of Jews missing in Europe. Their families looked for them in Israel by means of this program. The state is populated with the survivors of Hitler and their families. In the post-war years they poured into Israel by the hundreds of thousands. They stagnated for months and sometimes for years in makeshift reception camps until they could be provided with jobs and housing. Israel almost went bankrupt in absorbing the refugees but this absorption was Israel's *raison d'être* and it was never questioned. And the refugees salvaged whatever they could of their lives in Israel. And their children and grandchildren are born there and grow up speaking Hebrew and never know any country but Israel.

One wonders what would have become of the remnants of European Jewry had there been no Israel. We know that no other nation opened its door to the Jewish refugees. The American people opposed, eighty-three to eight percent, the admission of Jewish refugees to the United States. President Franklin D. Roosevelt himself vetoed the admission of ten thousand Jewish children to the bastion of democracy. A Treasury Department report, issued in 1944, indicted the United States Government not only for refusing to rescue Jews from Hitler but for going so far as to "prevent the rescue of these Jews." The report was entitled "Report to the Secretary on the Acquiescence of This Government in the Murder of the Jews." Britain, of course, closed Palestine to Jewish immigration in 1939 as the great pogrom was in its early stages. So much for the "democracies." So where could the Jewish refugees have gone in 1945? Back to Germany, Hungary and Poland? Recent history has shown how absurd any such proposal was. In post-war Poland there were pogroms in which Jews who had survived and returned "home" to Poland were massacred by their neighbors. Even today the threat of new pogroms and official government anti-Semitism is forcing the few remaining Polish Jews to leave that country. High-ranking Jewish communist officials in Warsaw, labelled Zionists, are forced to flee Poland for Denmark and Sweden.

There was no alternative to the creation of a state for the European Jewish refugees. (Later it would be shown that the Middle Eastern Sephardic Jewish community, in straits almost as desperate as the European community, also needed a refuge from anti-Semitism; so much so that in a few years it would compose a majority of Israel's people.) If there had been no Zionist movement prior to 1945 it would have developed in the wake of Auschwitz. In 1970 Israelis say *"ayn brera"* (no alternative) when asked about their current struggle. If that is so in 1970 it was even more so on May 15, 1948, when the members of the "National Council, representing the Jewish people in the Land of Israel and the Zionist Movement" proclaimed the "establishment of a Jewish State in the Land of Israel," a state for the refugees.

As such it seems incredible that twenty-two years later Israel has lost so much of the world's support. In 1948 all the forces of international progressivism welcomed the advent of Israel. Apparently all the nations were happy and relieved to see the Jews take control of their own fate. The creation of a Jewish State relieved the allies of the necessity of providing for the Jewish DP's and of any obligation of opening their own countries to them.

But today the element of guilt has evaporated. And the international left calls for liquidation of Israel. The Soviets liken Israel to Nazi Germany. And German leftists dust off Nazi propagandist Julius Streicher's anti-Semitic cartoons and use them against the "Fascist" Israelis. French leftists attack Jewish students and accuse them of the crime of Zionism. German students refuse to allow the Israeli Ambassador to speak on a German campus as the young Germans shout "Death to the Zionists." All this in the name of progressivism.

The left in America also has adopted the anti-Israel line. More subtle here, the radical students call for an end to Zionism and the establishment in Palestine of an Arab state where people "of the Jewish faith" will hold full minority rights. Jewish "revolutionaries," brought up in the comfort of Long Island or the San Fernando Valley, shout down kibbutz members and condemn them as "bourgeois," snicker at references to the Holocaust and solemnly assure each other that only the "Revolution" will solve the

Jewish problem. It is far from fashionable to support Israel. Even many of the radicals who do so must first assure themselves and their peers that they are not Zionists, and that although they support Israel's existence they view her government as unduly rigid and chauvinistic. Young supporters of Israel today do in fact apologize for that very support. That is a tragic indication of the success of the anti-Israel barrage.

Another measure of the success of the anti-Israel forces is the relative indifference of the overwhelming majority of Jewish students to the plight of Israel. These most political students who are the organizers of so much of the anti-war and anti-repression activity in the United States are so strangely quiet on the subject of the Middle East. These students who see every other issue in only the blackest and whitest of terms see the subject of Israel as strangely gray. Rightly opposing the imperialist adventures of the United States in Southeast Asia, they are much slower to judgment when the imperialist aggressor is the Soviet Union and, more importantly, are unmoved when the intended victim of said aggression is the Jewish State of Israel.

It is a measure of the singularity of the Jewish experience that only the Jews produce self-abnegating youth in the wake of success. The assimilationist Jew has always been with us, but it took the success of the Zionist dream to create in the diaspora a new breed of self-hating Jew. Not content to take the assimilation route through complete indifference to Jewish issues, the new assimilationists make their bid to join the majority society through open anti-Jewish identification. The cause of this development, as psychological as it is political, cannot be adequately assayed here, but the development itself cannot be overlooked.

But perhaps a contributing factor in this development lies in the apologetics and self-doubt that mark so much of pro-Israel argument today. Apparently the Jews are the only people who have to prepare rational and well-researched analyses, replete with quotes from everywhere, to explain why they have the right to exist. There is a school of radical, pro-Israel Jews who go to great lengths to prove that such luminaries as Ho Chi Minh, Fidel Castro and Eldridge Cleaver have, at one time or another, endorsed Israel's continued existence. That's very nice, and very irrelevant. There is much more evidence that indicates that the modern revolutionary heroes have been consistent opponents of Zionism, which in any case tells more about them than it does about us. The fact is that it is more than a little degrading for supporters of Israel to rationalize that support by comparing Zionism to any of the xenophobic national movements that are so popular with the left today. It would make much more sense if Eldridge Cleaver felt compelled to justify his movement by quoting from Ben-Gurion and Jabotinsky.

There is nothing for us to apologize about. What is called for is unabashed pride. The accomplishments of Zionism are singular and can well serve as a model for every oppressed and downtrodden people. A quick glance backwards should be convincing evidence that the achievement of the Zionist aim was little short of the miraculous. In 1897 Theodor Herzl organized the first Zionist congress. At its conclusion he wrote that "Today at Basle I founded the Jewish State." He added that if he said that publicly, at once, he would be universally ridiculed, but that in fifty years "everyone will perceive it." When Herzl recorded his prediction there were few Jews in desolate Palestine, there was no modern Hebrew language, the city of Tel Aviv had not yet been thought of and no representative of the Jewish "nation" was recognized or accepted anywhere. Herzl said in 1897 that in fifty years there would be a Jewish State. And fifty years later, in 1947, after the Holocaust that Herzl could not have foreseen, the

United Nations voted its support of the establishment in Palestine of the Jewish State of Israel. Today Jews determine their own destiny in their own land. Those who would add that Jews are still being killed and that Israel is no secure sanctuary should note that more of our people were killed in one hour at Babi Yar than have lost their lives in the twenty-two years of defending the State of Israel.

No Jew need rationalize his support of Israel. And if the existence of the Jewish State is a thorn in the side of the "Third World," then so be it. If the fact of Jewish self-rule in the Middle East serves "imperialist" interests, let it. If the survival of Israel complicates matters for Soviet and American cold war strategists, that is their problem. It is not ours. After Auschwitz it is not in our province to lighten the burden of the superpowers. They can continue their struggle over relative spheres of influence; Israel's struggle is for survival.

Every Jew must join Israel in that struggle. He must see that for the Jew nothing changes. As Marxists and international bankers, millions of Jews were murdered by Hitler and the Fascists. As Zionists, Jews are expelled from Poland and beaten in France. As imperialists, reactionaries and capitalists, Jews are being murdered by Soviet Russians and their Arab puppets. Yesterday we stood in the way of Hitler and had to be removed. Today we stand in the way of the Soviets. And tomorrow . . .

Tomorrow may see the victory of the "liberation" forces in Palestine. One day the Soviets cross the canal, the next day the Arabs invade Israel itself. Those who say that the "world" would never let it happen have not learned much.

One thing in that terrible apocalyptic vision of what must never happen but might is with me. On a hill in Israel, just outside Jerusalem, is a memorial museum called Yad Vashem. It is shaped like a crematorium. On its floor, starkly illuminated by flames, lie six million black tiles in which white tiles spell out the names "Auschwitz," "Dachau," "Bergen Belsen," "Buchenwald," "Treblinka" and the others. On that day when the progressive liberation forces of the anti-imperialists defeat Israel and succeed in "de-Zionizing" Palestine with the encouragement of all the revolutionary, anti-Zionist, emancipated Jews, what will happen as the conquerors climb that hill in Jerusalem to liberate Yad Vashem? One imagines that the universe would shake. One imagines that all life everywhere would stop. One imagines that it would mark the end of the world. But then one knows that it wouldn't.

Siah Lohamim *is more a phenomenon than a book, and Mark Braverman's essay is more than a review. The book is a collection of interviews and discussions with Israeli soldiers, presenting responses which are often startling in their revelations of sensitivity and humanity. Mark's thoughtful treatment of these conversations reflects the concern of many young American Jews that stereotypes of militaristic Israeli soldiers be discarded for a more balanced understanding of the complex morality with which participants in the Israeli-Arab war operate. Mark Braverman is a graduate of Columbia College, contemplating study in psychology and human development.*

The Jew as Conqueror:
The Hearts and Minds of Soldiers
in the Six-Day War*

by MARK BRAVERMAN

In English, *Siah Lohamim* would probably be rendered "Discussions with Soldiers," a title which serves to introduce the format of the book: a collection of interviews and panel-type discussions held in kibbutzim about two months after the 1967 Israeli-Arab war. The Hebrew, however, unusually rich in nuance, serves as a much better introduction to the contents. *Siah* can mean prayer, affliction, worries, contention in diversity. The prayers and anxieties of soldiers emerge as all these things at one time or another, and the advantage of the format is that the reader, as witness to the discussions, develops an affinity for many of the sentiments expressed.

The more than fifty or so interviews of three or four participants were conducted in the summer of 1967 in widely scattered kibbutzim. These interviews were pub-

* This selection originally appeared in *Response,* Vol. III, No. 1, Spring 1969.

lished by a "group of young members (*haverim ts'eerim*) of the kibbutz movement." (The first publication, in October 1967, was halted, and the second and third publications underwent some minimal censorship. I have the third edition.) Short essays and poems are scattered throughout. The language is of the spoken sort, with an abundance of elipses, dashes, repetitions and incomplete sentences. It takes a bit of getting used to, but, that done, the flavor of Israeli speech (those Anglicisms!) and manner comes through with wonderful directness, and the sometimes painful struggles with paradoxes and emotions are recorded with often jarring immediacy. More or less unedited, the discussions often focus on a single problem and then either veer off sharply to another topic or disintegrate disappointingly. Often the discussants seem to be on the verge of some great discovery of Jewish identity when someone is allowed to bring up a personal war experience which has little to do with the topic at hand. For the most part, the gems are either found in a sharp dialogue between two felicitously opposed figures, or in a lengthy monologue by someone with something substantial to say. Much is incoherent, there is the trivial and repetitive to wade through, but there is, at least, the virtue of genuineness.

The book cannot be considered a comprehensive social or cultural document. The material originates exclusively from the non-religious kibbutz, which represents less than four percent of the nation's people—an exclusive breed, an extreme one, some might even say. Would a similar book drawn from the cities be significantly different? What about one from the religious kibbutzim? What groups from within the state does *Siah Lohamim* represent? Who were the Morrocans, who the first generation, who the third? No, the book is drawn from the stereotyped Israeli —khaki shorts, "*tembel*" hat, non-religious and rough of speech, hard at work in the field when the shells began to explode around him. It is probably this very image that the

"young *haverim*" who initiated the effort wish to perpetu-
ate—but it is to their credit that they placed that image on
the line by making it face questions such as: What was
your reaction to the role of conqueror? Did you ever experience hate toward the enemy? Why must we always be
humanitarian? The value of the responses received is for
the reader to judge.

For an outsider the word "obsession" is hard to supress
when confronted with the Jew's continuing concern with
the relation of any event to its place in Jewish history. *Siah
Lohamim* is a case in point. Yoska, the parent of a soldier,
maintains that "there is a Jewish fate (*goral*) . . . the
Jew, even if he deny it, finds this fate. It pursues all who
flee from it!" Yoska pictures himself as Abraham the father: "We have educated our children to be ready for sacrifice—and now we have to pay for it" (he is referring to
the grossly disproportionate amount of casualties among
kibbutzniks). The war effort is pictured in terms of "such
an identification with the common fate that everyone was
ready to sacrifice all for it."

It is not hard to understand the development of such
an image. A small country, surrounded by enemies armed
by a great power, looks for strength to its history—a history
with its moments both of seemingly passive self-sacrifice
and of defiant resistance. Isaac lay bound on the altar in
May 1967. In terms of the "Jewish fate" it could have
gone either way.

One particular way that it had gone in recent history
haunted some soldiers particularly. Associations with the
Holocaust are, however, strangely ambivalent and hard to
pin down—somehow not fully enunciated, as if the soldiers themselves were not certain of their reactions and
associations. "We know what it is to see a people destroyed," writes Moki,

> perhaps that is why the world cannot understand us—
> our energy, and yet our hesitation. They do not under-

stand what it is to make war while being ashamed of fighting. The saying 'excuse us, we've won,' is not ironic —it is the case.

The experience of the Holocaust acts both as spur and rein. We must not be destroyed again, but in a bitter irony, we must thus become the destroyers. Moki's idea of "that Jewish sense of identification with sacrifices" seems to find expression in Asher's memories of the front in Sinai, watching Egyptian soldiers wander barefoot, aimless in the sands:

> Then, for some reason, there arose some association with the wanderings of the Jews in Europe and other places.

Good for you, Asher, choruses the humanitarian world. "But," continues Asher,

> Logically, one is immediately repelled by the idea. How can you compare. Dear God, how can you compare something like this?

On the simplest level, the Holocaust association serves to heighten sensitivity. "In my actions," says Kubi,

> the holocaust remained before me at all times. They killed us, destroyed us. Because of this everything was more intense (*harif*) for me. There were times when I thought I could not go on . . . there were things that reminded me of photos I had seen . . . stacked bodies . . .

This simple expression stands in contrast to the self-idealizing, almost pompous pronouncement of Moki or the self-flagellating associations of Asher. Asher, as seen by his own double take, is bothered by the suspicion of a pose. Yet he still goes on to describe how his primary association caused him to give the last of his water to the enemy soldiers.

From descriptions of Israel's treatment of the defeated

enemy, Moki's claims for "ashamed warmaking" do seem
to be borne out. Hagai tells of the captured field near Jenin
marked "mines" on an Israeli map.

> I was extremely impressed by the fact that there were
> no mines at all in the field. It was so marked so that the
> soldiers should simply not trample on the field.

Siah Lohamim abounds with such stories of Israeli officers'
attemtps to mitigate the harsh realities of war, and the essential agreement of troops with such actions. The entry
into Shechem, which was carried out without a shot and
hence resulted in the death of several comrades, is accepted by one discussant as a *modus vivendi* of Israeli
warmaking. There is a hesitation, an apology. However,
there is no delusion as to the nature of the enemy. The
book practically opens with Aharon's story of the hardware
salesman in the Galil who found that in the two week period of tension preceding the war he had been selling an
extremely large volume of heavy kitchen knives to Arabs.
Kubi, who had the Holocaust before him always, shud-
dered to think of the consequences of losing the war: "I
thought: what if it had been reversed . . . for they are
not men—I saw that by the way they had betrayed their
own country. If it had been reversed—they would have
been animals."

These hesitations, these reservations and self-analyses
on the part of some of the Israelis in the book can be quite
jarring. They jar us, who sat in front of our TV sets in Phil-
adelphia and followed Huntley and Brinkley's map of the
war as excitedly as we would the advance of a team on a
football field. It jars those who marveled at the skill of the
"pincer movement" on Jerusalem and who laughed in
pleasure at the irony of a successful Sinai campaign using
the exact strategy of 1956. The most shaken, however, are
those who find constant strength in their love of Jerusalem
and in their strong identification with Jewish history. For

them, the following interview might seem rather rude. They can find comfort, however, in the fact that, to the best of my knowledge, it is unique, finding a rather lonely place in *Siah Lohamim:*

> Amram: It is the historical ties—especially to Jerusalem. It was not clear to me before, but it is so clear to me now . . . these places must be ours.
>
> Rachel: Ours by what right? History? The Bible?
>
> Amram: Yes . . . yes . . . because it was once ours. . . .
>
> Aharon: I don't think that's the point at all. There exists a situation in which we wish to secure certain boundaries for this state, without which it is clear that we shall have no security. And it does not interest me or anyone whether it is ethical or not, because before this the area belonged to someone else . . . and afterwards came others and took it . . . and then we came again . . . such that it no longer matters.
>
> When we went up to fight in Jerusalem, we were not historical figures. And I think that this was the feeling of all: we were soldiers with a particular objective to accomplish.
>
> After the entrance through the Lion's Gate, when the *hevrah* had already reached the Western Wall and were pushing further against the snipers, and Rabbi Goren appeared there (he didn't impress anyone particularly), there appeared at the gate a group of four Arabs and a woman, and in a blanket they had a child. They did not say that it was a child—she was dead. They made a hole, placed her in it and covered the hole. I think that that was the moment that gave everyone—they call it a self-confrontation, involving a bit of human sensitivity, a lot more than from all the commotion there with the *shofars.*

Aharon refuses to recognize a historical dimension to the war, or to modern Israeli existence at all. His attitude serves to call much of the rhetoric and terminology which has surrounded the war into question: Perhaps the various ideological and historical "rewards" of the war, such as the possession of the Old City and increased security, are advanced at least in part to assuage that discomfort at the war's realities noted above. There are others who, although more reserved than Aharon, tried to disabuse themselves of any such suspicion. Amos, from Kibbutz Huldah, has just shocked everyone by stating that he is willing to visit the Western Wall only "as a peacetime tourist." He attempts to explain himself through the following story:

> A son from Huldah fell in the Syrian Heights. Several friends visited the parents. The mother cried. The father bit at his lips. Someone, trying to comfort them, said: "Look—at any rate, we have liberated Jerusalem . . . he did not die in vain." The mother broke down and said: "The entire Western Wall is not worth Micah's little finger. But if you tell me that we fought for existence—then surely it was worth it."

"It is possible to liberate men," continues Amos, "and for that it is worth it to die—but today I reject the myth of screaming land, and places crying out for liberation." Eli counters—but his tone is inscrutable:

> The entire country, all of the newspapers, talk about "liberation . . . we have reached such and such a place . . . they are ours . . . after two thousand years . . ." My friend wrote me a letter about his deep feelings upon reaching the cave of Mahpelah. But when I arrived I felt nothing.
> Uri: I don't know, I must tell you . . . I love Bible . . . and I learned about these things. When I reached ancient Jerico—the things which I had learned, history, Bible, archaeology, I tell you, this is my feeling . . . it was exactly like reaching, say, Montfort, and learning to recognize it as one should. It is mine. . . .

From this point, as is common in the book, the discussion de-intensifies, to a consideration of the difference between personal and group history. We would have liked to have heard Amos challenge Uri to follow his thoughts to their consequences in the light of the war.

Uri is typical of many in his acceptance of the status quo and in his enjoyment of the accruing benefits. "What have we," he would say, as does Nahman in an earlier discussion, "to be sorry over our victory? The catastrophe of victory, as it were!" Indeed, would reply Amos, a very catastrophe. Amos and others like him cannot accept the fact of having killed people for a cause which finally resulted in the acquisition of things they consider nonessential, i.e. anything besides *kiyum*. The word can mean any kind of existence or perpetuation. In Israel today it is a term meaning the continued physical preservation of the state. As far as I could see, no one contested this minimal justification of the war. *Kiyum* remains, and perhaps (who knows!) the fact of censorship might be recalled here, an unimpeachable principle. Amos: "We truly fought for our lives, and on that score there is no soul-searching and no second thoughts." But, this ideological point given, a new theme is sounded—that of tragedy. The very basis of Israel is not so much called into question as bemoaned. Nahman again:

> The war, in and of itself, is just. I say this because there are many who claim that Zionism itself is immoral and all that . . . and they go around with unclean consciences about the very fact of their existence in this land. But I don't know how it could have been done differently. Things developed as they did, and we came to these wars. And it is most tragic—tragic, but that is our lot. It is a hard lot.

But it goes deeper, this tragedy of Zionism. "It begins," continues Nahman,

> with the very essence of Zionism. The perpetuation of *Am Yisrael* and its chance to return to its own land is tied up with its oppression of those who lived here. If you were not to oppress anyone, they would still be

slaughtering you in the diaspora. I put it that crudely on purpose—don't think that I am happy to see sacrifices. We find ourselves in a terrible reality—terrible.

Nahman came to this conclusion when he was forced to realize that "justice is always with the strong. That is to say, there is no meaning in justice with no power to back it up. This is the cruel law of our age. I can only be sorry about it, but I am not willing to go around with a guilty conscience if I must realize my justice with force. I have no choice."

It is, of course, hard to take exception to Nahman's words. He seems to express well the problems of waging a "just war" and the terrible paradoxes inherent in such a term. We have seen how these paradoxes are manifested in some part in the way the war was carried out, and in some of the post-war attitudes of soldiers and parents. In the final analysis, however, the recognition of a paradox leaves one nowhere. The real problem is one that moves us into the future. Again, Nahman is its enunciator. "The big problem," he says,

> is the educational problem. How—with all the justification of this war from our point of view—not to become militarists and not to regard human life as a thing of less value or to become Arab-haters. How not to make our children into cynics who say, "Justice? There is no such thing! The U.N.—foolishness! Loyalty is relative." How to preserve values . . .

"Find three Jews and you have four opinions." Try as well to find two Jews who have the same idea of what Israel is to be in modern Jewish life, and your results will be similar. Whatever the "values" to be preserved in Israel are, however, whatever the state is to represent, produce and pursue, it is hopefully safe to assume that no one wants to see a land the preponderance of whose energies is devoted to military prowess and which exalts this as a desirable and valuable trait in its own right. But the problem of whether a country forced to fulfill the first part of that condition will have the second arrive in its wake is one which Nahman wisely recognized more than a year ago. One wonders what he thought at the 5728 Independence Day Parade, or at the Israeli Defense Forces exhibit outside Tel Aviv this fall. Please understand that I am not by any means advancing a ready-made interpretation of those events, nor am I trying to sneak a facile critique of Israel through the back door of indirect phraseology. What I would suggest is a look at the manifold cultural reactions expressed in any single event such as these. An Israeli friend of mine, my age, about twenty, was wounded seriously in the 1967 war and is serving in a top secret division of the army as a part of his regular term of service. This summer he spoke proudly and admiringly to me of the army as a vast, well-coordinated network, the biggest thing in Israel, and of his own experience as "very good for me, the thing which made me a man." I felt a bit queasy. I think that in any other situation, in another country, even my own, I would not have reacted so. But this was Israel, and although perhaps I have no right to be, I was more than normally sensitive to this kind of attitude. How much of this stress can a state as identity-conscious (it was founded on identity!) as Israel stand? I think I'm a little scared. The people in *Siah Lohamim* are. Perhaps we all are.

In the Spring of 1968, when Richard Narva wrote this piece, it seemed only a matter of time before the established Jewish organizations would be forced to forsake the norms of centralized control and paternalism which have informed so many of their activities in the student community. Yet most of the clamor which accompanied the Jewish community's crise de conscience over the failure of Judaism on the campus failed to materialize into efforts transcending rhetoric about "apathy" and "secular learning."

Richard claims that the roots of the problem lie in the fact that Judaism has been misrepresented to students, who have been organized into protective and self-defeating "junior congregations" by central organizations. A native of Boston, he was active in Jewish groups while attending Brown University, and in community organizing efforts in Providence. He is currently in the Coast Guard.

Judaism on the Campus
—Why It Fails*

by RICHARD NARVA

Elie Wiesel, perhaps the most eloquent witness to the Holocaust, dates all of history pre-Auschwitz and post-Auschwitz. The decade from the "final solution" to the establishment of the State of Israel marks an historical discontinuity for the Jewish people which has left world Jewry, in mourning and in the joy of returning to Zion, with a rekindled awareness of their unity as a people. Nevertheless, the end of the Jewish people in modern times is a much-discussed possibility, not as the ultimate conclusion of centuries of anti-Semitism (Auschwitz was that), but as a function of secularization in Western society. Both Jews and gentiles ask: Are Jews unable to preserve their particular community of belief and custom in

* This selection originally appeared in *Response*, Vol. II, No. 2, Fall 1968.

an open society whose principles or authority and overall value consensus are increasingly derived from secular sources?

No sub-community is more open or more secular than the modern university. An examination of Judaism on the campus, therefore, can provide both insight into Jewish community life in a secular social setting and the opportunity to focus upon the first generation of American Jews born after the decade of cataclysm—today's Jewish collegians—personally confronting the Judaism that is in America.

What are the distinguishing responses of contemporary Jewish college students toward Judaism on the campus? They are dissatisfaction and apathy—dissatisfaction with an unfulfilling Judaism and an apathetic non-participation in such a Judaism. Programmatically, the American university could provide an excellent setting for Jews to come to a mature developing understanding of their Judaism. But it does not.

The onus of this article is to put forth reasons for the failure of contemporary Judaism on the campus to attract student commitment, to examine what the more general consequences of this specific failure may be for the American Jewish community, and in conclusion, to offer a program for renewal. It is necessary immediately to add that in my opinion neither organizational reform, nor programmatic revision, nor even massive transfusions of capital are sufficient to remedy this situation. No less than a radical rethinking and restructuring of Judaism on the campus is needed. And if commitment to such a basic review and renewal emerges among both students and the Jewish establishment, but only if it does, less than massive funds will be required to begin a concrete program.

The sharp focus of this paper is not those Jews who follow the ways of their fathers (whatever kind of Jew that father may be) without question. Rather it concerns those to whom Judaism is problematical, those self-aware intellectuals, who, though born into the Jewish community, find themselves in tension with that community. While it is no revelation to indict Jews in America for caring more about a plethora of organizational forms than the content of Jewish life in this country, it is exactly this commonplace that is the root of Jewish failure on the campus. The function and temper of the university (at least for the undergraduate) is a concern for ideas. It is logical, then, to assume that the university would be the first place where deep dissatisfaction with the well-formed, but meaningless kind of Judaism we have in America would surface. And it is incredibly evident, especially among those Jewish students most intellectually able, that contemporary American Judaism so dominated by what Elie Wiesel calls "executive directors," whose establishment fails to grant any real respect to the authority of genuine spiritual and intellectual leaders, has produced exactly this result all across the American college scene.

The current Jewish establishment—most second generation Jews—followed a classic pattern which lies at the root of their apparent inability to see how they produce the serious failure of Judaism on the campus: first, a forsaking of part or all of their Judaism in order to become more American, and secondly, a later determination that their children should not do the same. A severe intergenerational conflict particular to this historical situation occurs when the parents (second generation) urge their children onto greater Jewish identification than they themselves evidence, saying in effect, "Do as I say, not as I do." The reality which must undergird all Jewish education of our generation is that we know neither the experience of the second generation, marginality, nor that of the first, Judaism as a way of life. To us, today in the United States, Judaism has become an ancillary set of commitments to a basically American way of life. Family religious occasions,

Sunday school, the synagogue, summer camp, and for our purposes here, Hillel too are used to *forge* young Americans *into* Jews. Such molding is the mandatory price of Jewish life within open society. But it is a new process more involved with the gut problem of preserving Jews than with the quality of Judaism so preserved.

If we continue with the premise that Jewish teenagers go to college in huge numbers, seventy-five to eighty percent in fact, then the failure of Judaism on the campus means that the forging mechanism breaks down precisely at the most crucial period in their intellectual training. For those students to whom college is primarily vocational preparation this situation is not so grievous. And this group is not small since eveyone knows that young Jews go to college not only because learning is an ancient Jewish tradition, but also because a university degree is the key to upward social mobility. But when one considers the matter of the quality of future Jewish leadership then the problem emerges in its most serious perspective. One cannot avoid asking: "On what grounds can it be assumed that sensitive, responsible young adults, coming from homes where the parents have followed the classic second generation pattern, who have received an inadequate Jewish education, will be motivated to enter into the American Jewish community in any serious fashion?" If Judaism remains only a stagnant inheritance from childhood with less vitality than the life of the university, then *the most vital element* of Jewish youth will no doubt slough it off with the rest of adolescence.

Looking at the status of Judaism on the campus in some detail, one finds that the organization is obsolete, that its program priorities are off target, and that its very goals do not coincide with the substantive concerns of the current campus population. Year after year Jewish organizations fail to articulate the demands of the rising number of Jewish collegians, and fail more importantly to provide a locus for training Jewish leadership. Most tragic of all is the consequent lack of opportunity for Jewish students to confront the problem of their Jewish identity in tension with a vital Jewish community. If it is a worthwhile goal to spur Jews with strong secular backgrounds into a confrontation with their Judaism, and I think this must be a primary goal in our time, then the current situation simply will not do.

Present campus alternatives hardly appear to be the answer. Understaffed, overworked Hillel *de facto* devotes its time and energy to the most traditional students. As a result the rest of the students too often unwilling to swallow Hillel's hard line and rabbinical domination take their talents elsewhere. The quality of Jewish community life in the Jewish fraternities is hardly the primary concern of the Greeks. There are few other alternatives; departments of Judaic studies provide instruction, but not the motivation for Jewish literacy. These are not condemnations, but the hard facts of college life. The campus Jewish community is stagnant at the same time that Jewish students are hyperactive elsewhere. If the situation is to change new goals must be set, basic programming reworked and new student institutions established.

The goals can be briefly stated: first, a renewed concern for the quality of Jewish life for *all the Jews* on campus; second, a corporate engagement with social problems; third, Jewish student responsibility for Jewish student affairs, including fiscal affairs; and fourth, the maintenance of a journal and sponsorship of projects of high intellectual caliber for the expression and information of Jewish collegians. Forging such a renewal of course raises many questions. Most involve the word "how."

First of all, how should Judaism on the campus be organized? There is a good model in the burgeoning new University Christian Movement. The most essential word in the name for our purpose is "movement." For though there is national administrative structure UCM is substantively different from conventional religious organizations. Nationally and locally it has emerged as a result of student effort; it exists as the concrete expression of the "Christian" needs of a growing number of students. The hallmarks of UCM are interdenominational union and social and political activism—two policies which reveal both the lack of other religious organizations and the foremost concern of many religiously identifying Christian college students. No one imposes UCM on a campus; the students themselves create it.

In the case of Jewish students, I do not mean to argue that a campus Jewish organization must become a subsidiary of UCM or that it must de-mythologize, disband and give its money and members to SDS. I do mean to argue that a campus Jewish organization that is embarrassingly silent on major issues of concern to students can become an actual block to Jewish identification. In this case a national policy made in Washington and imposed by fiat is in direct contradiction to the commitment these same Jewish students personally make. All talk of Judaism being relevant to the issue is hogwash if no corporate Jewish body on the campus can make its presence felt.

Structurally, then, a common denominator exists between all campus religious groups, namely, that they must come to terms with the setting of a university: with a population of generally high intellectual capacity, with a new spirit of activism, with the intense competition among organizations for the students' free time; in sum, with the factors within a predominantly secular community that influence what the people in that community do with their time. Religious identification through campus religious organization is no automatic matter. Thus, the structural, program, staff and financial needs of campus religious organizations, regardless of faith, are more alike than those of campus Jewish groups and other organizations in the extended Jewish community.

Such a new movement would raise significant problems regarding the existing Jewish organizations on campus. Could Hillel and a new Jewish movement exist simultaneously on a college campus? I would say that in the formative stages of the movement group—yes; but only temporarily. There is, as I have already explained, evidence that Hillel presents a structural block to the formation of a significant or meaningful Jewish group on some campuses. In a political battle with Hillel (which would be inevitable) Hillel's paid staff and facilities would be useless assets. A new Jewish movement would have only one strength—it would not exist unless its members brought it into existence. It would grow insofar as its members sought new ways to express Judaism on the campus. It would succeed like any idea shared by eager adherents whose creativity and independent action are not frustrated by absentee authority.

How is Judaism on the campus to be led? The result of excluding Jewish students from positions of responsibility for their own affairs, from policy making and fiscal control, is the virtual write-off of any opportunity to recruit talented students seeking challenges equal to their abilities. A major implication of my proposals, therefore, is a re-definition of the role of the rabbi on the campus. Briefly, I believe that he should be a chaplain and no more, since quite naturally the students will *de facto* make of him more than the average campus clergyman (if he merits such increased status by his own example). As counselor, teacher and friend his role will not change. But as a model for his leadership role the Hillel counselor is more appropriate than Hillel director. In fact, if, as defined by a new movement, the responsibilities of the positions are diminished, a faculty member, especially in Judaic studies, might be more effective.

Jewish students on today's campus, hitherto organized on a junior congregation model, are rejecting this patronizing situation as the percentage of Jewish students active in Hillel across the country indicates. If students can be responsible for the entire student activities budget at Brown, for curriculum reform and numerous other major tasks at the university, then they are certainly capable of managing their own campus Jewish life.

How would financing work? There can be no integrity for any new Jewish movement without fiscal integrity. Money must come the most difficult way, with no ideological strings attached. There will, no doubt, be programs of such a movement that the Jewish establishment, qua establishment, considers radical or controversial. If the movement is bound to the umbilical cords of dollars there will obviously be no such programs, and thus there is no reason to begin—no reason unless there is trust from the donors that the student recipients are competent to manage their own affairs.

Previously rigidified lines of distribution must be re-examined and new lines opened to allocate resources to meet the new problems of Judaism and the third generation. B'nai B'rith's monopoly on funding Hillel is more than anachronistic, it is dysfunctional, preventing much needed funds from reaching the campus. Breaking that monopoly is essentially a political matter for the establishment. Meanwhile local community funds, which often supply the bulk of local Hillel revenue, could become the primary source of support for the new movement once seed capital is raised. But as the freedom movement and the resistance reveal: to translate an ideal into action commitment is far more important than large budgets; the type of commitment that does not tolerate foolish bureaucracy.

Finally, what will be the program priorities of a new Jewish movement? No statement about programming can be considered realistic until the incredible apathy of Jewish students to Jewish activities on campus is recognized. Such apathy, while rooted in the secular temper of the university, is terribly increased by the mediocrity of current programming. There simply are too many better things to do than associate with a Jewish organization for all the reasons already discussed. Nevertheless, each year a new crop of interested talent enters fresh from the hometown forge ready to activate the collegiate Jewish community anew, ready that is, until they experience the disillusionment of driving a tin lizzie in a Grand Prix race. But given that Judaism has a new vehicle, what programs should be presented?

Certainly the dietary facilities, worship schedule and seminars in traditional Jewish sources should continue. But why not experiment as a matter of policy? It is not possible to vary worship patterns in most adult congregations, whether traditional or liberal, but on campus new readings, new melodies, from traditional sources, from nontraditional sources, even whole new services written by students would both provide challenges to creative students and stimulate re-examination of the tradition. Indeed the new movement could sponsor colloquiums on creative liturgy, regionally and nationally. Attendance at Jewish study groups would be more than a handful if such study was either relevant to the gut issues of the students' lives—the draft, racism in America, Vietnam and violence in general—and/or if Jewish students lobbied for more departments of Jewish studies so that they could get academic credit for their effort. However, to obviate the need for a single-minded reading of the sources, not only study groups, but Judaism as a corporate entity must emerge from its silence and into the real world.

The American Jewish establishment must realize that if it is going to maintain a Jewish campus community this community cannot be divorced from social involvement. More conservative (in religious matters) Jewish students must also grant this latitude to the hitherto closed Hillel program. Much of the best Jewish talent, albeit not always extremely literate in Judaica, enters campus radical groups because of their Jewish upbringing (see Kenneth Kenniston's *Young Radicals*), and because of a concern for human dignity and social justice learned from our tradition. Alienation of Jewish intellectuals can only be increased by the current situation of campus Judaism. Probably the negative experience generated is more harmful than having no Jewish organization at all.

A renewal of Judaism at the nation's colleges and universities according to the basic guidelines presented in this article is not a panacea, nor a utopian dream. It is a basic concrete program to provide Jews of the third generation with a much needed opportunity to confront the problem of their Jewish identity.

In these remarks to his fellow Hillel directors, Rabbi Albert Axelrad reveals that the kind of critique of campus Judaism presented by Richard Narva in the preceding essay has not always fallen on deaf ears. In this essay we are provided with an insight into one young rabbi's sympathetic response to young Jews who have been alienated by traditional religious structures on the campus, but who are nevertheless willing to struggle with tensions they experience as Jews.

Rabbi Axelrad, Jewish Chaplain and Adviser to students at Brandeis University, is not interested here in winning campus radicals back into a static "Jewish fold"; he argues to his colleagues that there is much which the sensitivity and ethos of radicals can contribute toward the development of a viable campus Jewish life-style. He believes that many young Jews are willing to confront the aspects of Jewish experience, negative and positive, which he claims engage them.

A graduate of Hebrew Union College (Reform), Rabbi Axelrad has been active in many of the radical campaigns and causes of his students.

Encountering the Jewish Radical: The Challenge for Campus Rabbis and Student Groups

by ALBERT S. AXELRAD

Much is spoken and written today about the Jewish identity of college students; sociologists, political scientists, historians, rabbis, and other actual or self-styled experts have written a considerable amount on the subject. The results of their surveys and studies seem to indicate that the overwhelming majority of Jews on the campus do not identify themselves actively as Jews, and that, in all, Jewish continuity on the campus is in a state of crisis.

Unfortunately many of these reports—which are often characterized by hyperbole, a desire for the sensational, and sometimes by self-seeking interpretations—fail to offer a comprehensive and therefore meaningful understanding of the situation.

They generally fail, for instance, to reflect the fact that the lack of Jewish involvement on the part of students often represents not alienation but a desire to "get perspective." For many young people the process of growing up requires stepping back from value systems and identifications often imposed upon them by their elders in early years. The campus atmosphere encourages this kind of detachment.

This is not to say that stepping back is always necessary; in fact it may be necessary only in direct proportion to the extent to which the religious atmosphere of a person's earlier years has been stifling and coercive. Nor is stepping back always the prelude to permanent detachment. There is often a return to a Jewish identification and a religious life altogether different from the earlier parental pattern (hopefully different, I would add, in most cases). We must understand the potential importance of such a temporary retreat for the emotional and spiritual development of many students.

Many of the reports also fail to understand that where alienation exists, the damage is usually done long before a student reaches the campus. I refer to such obvious alienating factors as the passivity of many segments of the Jewish community in social and political arenas, the community's often-manifested tendency for flamboyance, its self-absorption and lack of receptivity to change, its seemingly primary commitment to survivalism for its own sake. And I refer especially to the victimization of the young at the hands of the wretched Jewish educational systems that exist in many communities.

By the time they enroll in college, then, many students are already estranged from Jewish life. If there is any cause for alarm, it is in connection with the established Jewish community's organization and priorities.

Of course many students come to the campus more positively identified with Jewish life, and they maintain this commitment throughout their college careers. It is certainly a responsibility of the campus rabbi and of student-directed Jewish groups to help provide the vehicles through which they may continue to express and deepen their commitment.

But I think there is an equally great responsibility to encounter and respond to those students who are alienated, especially those who consider their sympathy with the social and political left to be ideologically incompatible with Jewish commitment. I say this because there is increasing evidence in my experience that it is the alienated themselves who find themselves open to and desirous of some serious confrontation with Jewishness.

Obviously there are young Jews who are exceedingly negative in their attitudes toward Judaism; my own impression is that this group is not excessively large and that it hardly characterizes all or even most Jews on the left. Assuming that self-hatred is uncomfortable and confusing at the very least, attempts by campus rabbis and other groups to encounter this hostility among Jewish radicals might be worthwhile.

In the main, however, I am concerned with the Jewish radicals who are, in varying degrees, positive yet confused about their Jewish identity. Confusion, more than antipathy, is the leitmotif in the Jewish identification of most campus radicals. The confusion is occasioned by tensions which tug at radical Jewish students (and frequently also faculty members) from several directions simultaneously. Among the most consequential are:

1. *Personal social commitment versus Jewish communal apathy.* In most cases students' radicalism is principled and courageous. Many of them may not realize that their social values can be more easily squared with Judaism than can the values of most Jewish communal institutions and their leaders.

2. *Universal humanism versus particularism.* Many radicals do not reject the particular as a form of identity, except insofar as it conflicts with universal and humanistic concerns. These students may wish to use the particular as a point of departure. They do not consider nationalism or group survival important for their own sake; they consider Jewish nationalism to be no less invidious than any other kind, except as it becomes a vehicle for the implementation of certain values. Even black nationalism is seen by them only as a temporary necessity reflecting a situation of "crisis and combat identity."

3. *Empathy for Israel versus the radical Third World critique.* This tension is an aspect of the conflict between the universal and the particular, but it deserves special treatment. Many Jewish radicals do empathize with Israel, but their loyalty is not blind. They are not convinced that Israel is completely blameless for the Middle East impasse. They are fearful of the possibilities of Jewish chauvinism and militarism. Sometimes they are susceptible to propaganda which simplistically links Israel with American imperialism, and disregards the progressive, socialistic tendencies manifested in Israel's internal life and in her aid programs to Africa and South America. But most of all, they are offended by what appears to be the irrational, close-minded stance of the American and Israeli Jewish establishment, which fails to separate legitimate criticism from "anti-Semitism."

4. *Privatism in religious expression versus the search for community.* I do not find that radical Jews are necessarily "anti-religious." Many yearn for religious experience, but through individualistic and private rather than conventional and institutional channels. At the same time,

however, there is often a yearning for community as an aspect of religious search. Few and far between are the Jewish responses to both needs.

Some of these tensions are relatively new. Certainly their simultaneous convergence and impact on campus is a recent phenomenon. My guess is that the group of campus Jews most sensitive to these tensions is growing in size. Regardless of their numbers, Jewish radicals who are "positive but confused" about their Jewishness include some of the most idealistic, moral, articulate, sensitive, and creative students on the campus. The prophetic ideal characterizes them much more than it does the adult Jewish community.

I have suggested that one of the responsibilities of campus rabbis is to "encounter" these students. I use the term "encounter" deliberately, despite its ambiguity. Let me attempt to give it specific meaning, both ideologically and programmatically.

To encounter someone is to meet him where he is rather than to bring him to where you are. To do the latter is to proselytize, to fail to consider the individual, his unique humanity, his needs and well-being. To "encounter" Jewish radicals is to take seriously and sympathetically their values and ideals, their hassles and tensions, and to participate with them in reconciling and resolving these on their own ground, *if they are concerned to do so*, rather than trying to attract them to conventional services, observances, and fund drives. Our responsibility is to provide an arena in which radicals can, with some availability of Jewish knowledge, deal with the tensions I've described.

What are the programmatic implications? As a beginning, the campus rabbi should attempt to make his sympathetic presence felt in the gatherings and causes of radicals. This may not be easy; he may suspect that he is being used by radicals, and radicals may suspect that an attempt is being made to co-opt them and their energies into the religious and other establishments.

He should, where possible, dissolve the apparent tension between radical social commitment and Jewish commitment. Attention should be called to the existence of Jewish activist and radical groups which do not shrink from taking leftist and militant positions on various matters, general and Jewish. The prophetic imperative is clearly able to contribute precedent and perspective to many popular radical stands regarding war, racism, and exploitation.

With regard to the tension between universalism and particularism, he might at minimum ask for understanding of the Soviet Jewish problem (to cite only one example) not in isolation, but as an instance of human oppression and persecution; and he would view in equally sympathetic fashion the cries of other oppressed and persecuted peoples.

To the extent that the tension between loyalty to Israel on the one hand and to the Third World on the other is an aspect of the universal-particular tension, young Jews might approach the problems of the Middle East through fund drives that support Arab-Jewish rapprochement, and which alleviate Arab and Jewish suffering. They might organize campus "cells" which bring together visiting Arabs, Israelis, locals, and others, in order to initiate ongoing dialogue on the Arab-Jewish impasse. They should support the efforts of the nascent Israeli left, and have contact with its periodicals, and its representatives when they visit the United States.

The tension between religious privatism and the search for community ought to be confronted through the creation of informal religious fellowships meeting in non-institutional surroundings; through the popularization and study of religious personalities from the prophets to the modern writers; and through the rediscovery of mystic and communal trends in Jewish life and history, such as Hasidism. Radical Jews sensitive to the spirit of these trends and traditions in their own past might profitably shed some of their alienation and ahistorical Jewish perspective by experimenting with encampments or retreats.

Presumably, in all of these areas, the knowledge and assistance of the campus rabbi and other knowledgeable Jews will prove useful. Hopefully these personalities will learn to make themselves available, both as spurs and participants.

Whether the rabbi devotes most of his energy to this kind of encounter or to the maintenance of more conventional vehicles of expression will depend upon his orientation and inclinations, on his understanding of Jewish imperatives, on his sense of Jewish needs and priorities, and on the extent to which he himself is sympathetic to Jewish radicals. But in any case, students of all leanings should be met as individuals, rather than as potential converts to a particular program or viewpoint.

Those who would be interested in creating a radical Jewish life-style should not be dissuaded by the relative absence of such an option in the adult Jewish community (notable exceptions including Jews for Urban Justice and the *havurot*); they have a right to the services and knowledge of the rabbi, who can help them to build that lifestyle.

Encounter with radicals in search of a viable Jewishness will require strong decentralization of the Jewish campus community. Radicals and traditionalists may not be very compatible (although there are many dramatic exceptions), the former wanting only the loosest and most tenuous connection with the organized Jewish community. Neither should have anything resembling a veto power over the positions or programs of the other.

More money, resources, and time for campus rabbis are as important as willingness to decentralize. As things stand, we are pulled in all directions with our responsibilities for religious services, observances, study groups, service projects, lectures, action groups, personal, draft, and religious counseling, and involvement in campus crises. We are grossly understaffed, overwhelmed with students, causes, and programs, and unwisely ignored on the monetary level by fund raisers and Jewish communal leaders who place communal "defense" and public relations above the needs of university populations.

That Jewish radicalism is distasteful to some campus rabbis is unfortunate. When I entered Hillel, it was made lucidly clear to me that, regardless of a rabbi's personal predilections, he was to be hospitable to Jews of all "persuasions." My experience is that the rubrics "orthodox," "conservative," and "reform" no longer encompass the spectrum of "persuasions" to which we must be hospitable, since many young Jews concerned with Judaism do not find themselves comfortable with these positions and labels. The new reality invites us to include the radical along with the more traditional Jews; it asks us to respond to his tentative probings.

Certainly these considerations, if implemented, would change the image of Jewish campus groups from that of centers for traditional worship, or kosher eating clubs, or Jewish fraternities and sororities, to that of centers for the creation of a Jewishness that is exciting to a broader spectrum of students. But, more importantly, encounter as I have tried to describe it—without proselytizing—is the only moral way of interacting with individuals. Further, it is perhaps the only way of offering to the young Jew a chance to bring Jewish knowledge and sensitivity to bear upon the tensions he experiences because of his Jewishness. And encounter might conceivably provide the necessary atmosphere of trust and the required stimulus for the creation of an indigenous Jewish life for American activists and radicals.

Jewish education in an open society cannot merely attempt to initiate the young into a religious style which is unresponsive to their needs and experiences as secular Americans. As participants in modern man's crisis of faith and quest for meaning, the American Jewish young embody a fundamental challenge not only to the techniques and styles of Jewish education, but to the essence and content of the Jewish experience which that education tries to transmit.

In this essay, James Sleeper argues that a purpose of Jewish education should be to encourage and support a creative, radical alienation from much of American life. He suggests that this goal, which presupposes a strong student-teacher relationship and tries to nurture spiritual and prophetic communities, is grounded in the tradition; desperately needed by an American society in crisis; demanded by youth's deepest yearnings and most pressing needs; and tactically indispensable to building a Jewish community and a Jewish historical role worth preserving.

In confronting these claims, we have an opportunity to move beyond the dull stereotypes and negative associations related to Jewish education with which many of us have been burdened, and to project an American Jewish future for ourselves and for our children which we could heartily endorse, not reluctantly maintain.

Authenticity and Responsiveness in Jewish Education

by JAMES A. SLEEPER

*Why Modern Jewish Education
Must Begin outside the Tradition*

Once upon a time, Jewish parents had no more to decide to give their children a sense of Jewish identity or a working Jewish education than modern American parents have to decide that their children shall speak English; Jewishness was absorbed into the young person's growing identity and self-image as he developed in the midst of a viable, organic Jewish community. In fact, he had no alternative but to express both his deepest needs and his most casual preferences through the media of Jewish symbology and language. One did not have to speak of this young person's "commitment" to Jewish values—a term implying attachment to something which one might also ignore or reject. Values were absorbed as a natural by-product of immersion in a culture, where words like *tzedakah* (which is not really "charity") and *rachmonus* (which is not really "mercy") came to describe rich and complex human relationships which were entered into as second-nature responses to all kinds of situations and predicaments.

Our purpose here is not to romanticize such a *gemeindschaft,* or all-inclusive community, as this, or to suggest that modern Americans can or should return to the all-embracing cultural and mythical climate which has been perhaps forever destroyed. Rather, it is to provide a perspective, a backdrop against which to view the dilemma of Jewish educators who operate today *without* the support of such a community. It is to suggest that as soon as identification with one's people becomes something that is self-conscious, principled, and purposeful, it is a whole new ball game.

Whatever its roots in the eighteenth-century *Haskalah,* or enlightenment, the problem is basically a new one. For even members of the current "older generation" spent at least their formative years in some kind of contact with the transplant of the closed ghetto community their parents tried to carry over from Europe; accordingly, they, no less than our mythical young person of ages past, find that one of the primary components of their socialization and self-image is the *pintele yid,* that ineradicable sense of Jewishness which surfaces at least occasionally to create havoc with carefully calculated loyalties and elaborately reasoned postures on the American scene. It is really their children, members of the current "younger generation," who are the first, en masse, to have had no primary Jewish cultural experiences.

One might dismiss hostility toward the Jewish community and Jewish self-hatred on the part of some of these young people as reflective of sickness or adolescent trauma. But the fact remains that many young Jews simply dismiss Jewishness with a shrug that is neither spiteful nor reflective of any particular personal difficulty. Put simply, in the wake of the old community's collapse they have almost no memories, no primary associations with even the glimmer of a viable, organic Jewish community in which Jewish language, symbols, and values were compellingly operative during their early years. Nothing *recognizably Jewish* makes them what they are. Why, then, should they recognize themselves as Jews?

In the absence of the organic community, the Jewish classroom is charged with the impossible responsibility of providing emotional attachment to Jewishness, and with setting up a socializing arena in which Jewish "values" may be acted out, Jewish symbols employed as natural reflexes to the broad spectrum of a day's activities and secret moments. Somehow the Jewish school is expected to "reach out" to the essentially non-Jewish student, in a language foreign to the tradition, across a widening cultural and philosophical chasm. It is doubtful that even the most extravagantly budgeted and hardwared classroom can do these things; flannel boards and opaque projectors do not mold Jews. Nor, alas, do inquiry and classroom "discussion." The epitome of classroom inquiry was reached in one college Judaica course I attended, in which an assimilated young academic exclaimed over his study of Jewish history, "Amazing! A civilization whose religious values are so well expressed in a cultural matrix, in which every symbol has a divine referent!" He stayed assimilated, rational insight alone not being the stuff of which growth, self-authentication, or commitment are made.

Hence, the first elementary thesis of this paper: Even granting a measure of integrity to Jewish life and tradition, any discussion of Jewish *education* must begin with a discussion of the fundamentally *non*-Jewish context in which our students have developed as human beings. The would-be Jewish educator (which I hope to show is something more than "Jewish academic") must know the world in which his students move (which I hope to show is something more than "know about" that world), if he is to address them uncompromisingly with the riches of Jewish tradition, and if he is truly to become a meeting point of student and tradition.

The Search for a Meeting Point

Religious commitment in our time is not a product of academic inquiry alone, whether literary, sociological, or philosophical. Erikson and others have suggested that it is a complex, organic meeting of a growing, need-filled individual with the ongoing symbols, values, and language of a religious tradition. The student gravitates toward that tradition, tries on its symbols as a means of personal expression, struggles to reconcile his inclinations with its value judgments, encounters its moments of holiness and prayer as shimmering and precious arenas of love and trust, only if that tradition addresses him in his present state, only if it offers meaningful personal satisfactions, only if it meets his conscious and unconscious needs for community and self-definition. What to do when his present state, his conscious and unconscious needs were nurtured in a non-Jewish environment, when his values conflict with those of the tradition, when he speaks, even if only half-heartedly, the language of "charity" and "mercy"?

One option is to emphasize the "relevance" of the tradition to his present world, to bend and twist it to be compatible with his values and whims. I doubt that this will make it seem very interesting or attractive, especially if he is unhappy with his current situation. We are not interested in raising Judaism's hemline, in watering down her claims to make them compatible with American culture; indeed, to respond to the pull of our history and tradition is to feel increasingly uncomfortable with much of what is happening in America (and you can bet I'm not speaking only of what may be happening among "antinomian" participants in "youth culture"; we may also have a rather mindless and antinomian government, a plastic culture, and an economic system which unwittingly destroys communities and corrupts interpersonal relationships).

What is more, demonstrations of Judaism's compatibility with American life are pathetically uninteresting because increasing numbers of Jewish teenagers are themselves uncomfortable with their governmental, cultural, and economic surroundings. It is ironic for the Jewish educator to despair, as one did at a recent conference, of "ever introducing some American kid off the streets to the meaning of *kedusha* [holiness]," when he has only to go into the streets to find a generation which grants a wider margin of credibility to the craving for this dimension of human experience than did its parents. I am not claiming that astrology and the occult describe a movement toward Jewish tradition; they describe merely a yearning, and an open door, the awareness of a vacuum in the religious life of the society into which the young have been initiated.

If yearning and openness are to be converted into satisfying personal growth and religious movement, if the Jewish experiences of *kedusha, tzedakah,* and *rachmonus* are to become compellingly attractive to these young people, they will have to encounter Jewish religious life operating as a vital force inside of living people whom they trust, and who are conversant with their "hassles," dilemmas, and often unconscious and unarticulated needs. My own experience is that the Jewish educator who would serve as such an example can hardly afford to be condescending about it; for all his credentials, he is likely to discover that he has as much to learn from the young about the rejuvenation of religious dimensions in daily life as they have to learn from him.

The greater variety of models who radiate enthusiasm

about some form of contact with Judaism, the better. As things stand now, of course, it is highly unlikely that the student in the Jewish school will meet even one such person in all his years of religious education. The reasons bear repetition: there is no viable, organic, operative Jewish community to nurture such models; there is no setting in which Jewish language, symbols, and values are publicly articulated, shared, celebrated, and employed to embrace the experiences of the young. The controversial *havurot* are at least halting bootstrap operations in the creation of such communities, which may explain in part why *havurah* members who serve as Hebrew school principals and teachers in the greater Boston and New York City areas seem to enter their classrooms with an authenticity which has proved to be compellingly attractive to their students. Because *havurah* members embrace youth culture in order to transform it, they are excellent meeting points between the young and the tradition. (The spectacle of critics remote from the scene projecting their own worst demons and fears onto the "promiscuous," "psychedelic," and "underground" activities of these groups would be cause for a great deal of amusement were it not so potentially damaging to the first fragile glimmer of Jewish educational success we have seen in some time.)

Jewish authenticity on the part of the teacher is indispensable; and we should not lower our standards regarding to his Jewish knowledge. But authenticity and scholarly knowledge are insufficient. They must be coupled with a responsiveness to our students, with a willingness to approach them in a way that is other than condescending or therapeutic. That does not involve self-compromise as much as it demands a great deal of openness and energy, as well as the readiness to take seriously the maxim that "from my students I learned most of all."

Truly to know the young Jews of suburbia is to see them in their natural habitats, and on their own turf, and only then to see even more in them than they themselves do. It is to see in their often self-defeating experiments intimations of health and strength as well as of sickness; hints of religious growth and awakening as well as of myopic preoccupation with occult escapes; gifts of prophecy as well as of nihilism. Finally, to know the young is to expose oneself to fundamental and lasting change, for in their questions and their life-styles lie challenges to the tradition so fundamental that they reflect more than the perspective or the problems of the young alone.

The young Jews of whom I will speak are not necessarily representative of the bulk of American youth. Hence they will be viewed by some as deviant in a negative sense from an orderly and healthy society whose most serious mistake is to have overindulged them, thereby creating for itself an elitist nuisance. I prefer to view them as a sort of barometer, as a group whose alienation and searching bespeak a societal crisis and sickness which they have not caused but are trying with increasing desperation to avert or escape.

It goes without saying that the truth lies somewhere in between; certainly the young are no more righteous, no less the victims of materialism and other social ills than are the members of the "establishment" they attack. The point is that, not yet having an economic or political or personal stake in the going system, they are more free to question it, to become aware of distorted values and priorities which they have begun—but not finished—internalizing and living out.

A value-laden psychoanalytic critique of the young which preferred to remain blithely ignorant of its own rootings in Victorian norms, and which left social irritants largely unexamined, would paint them primarily as sick, negative deviants. But please understand that once you accept the framework of psychoanalysis, *all* views are subject to its scrutiny—not only the protestations and experiments of the young, but also the directives and policies of their elders. The antinomian behavior of the young is a priori no more deserving of psychoanalytic comment than is the morality they seem to oppose. Were I to describe the behavior of some members of the "older generation" as bizarre in that they speak with reticence about sexual matters, their dress is fastidious, their hair close-cropped, and their consumption of barbiturates and alcohol conspicuous, I believe I could make my point. The views of the young are no more energized by psychic needs than are the views of their academic and professional and political critics. We have often been told that the young radical is playing the part of the son in the oedipal conflict. Is no one playing the part of the father?

A Preliminary Sketch of Youthful Discontent

First, let us have some of the students I have known speak for themselves, and let us share some of their favorite song lyrics. The reader may do with this material what he wishes—one option, at least, is to take it somewhat at face value.

> Everywhere I go I wear masks; at home I'm the dutiful son, at school the performing student; nobody asks for more. The only place I can really be "me" is when I just drop out with a couple of friends. So you might say that my real life is underground.
>
> (age 16)

> I feel as if there's a tender flower inside me which grew, hoped, wanted to be loved and to give, and then wilted and died.
>
> (age 18)

> I always wear shades [dark glasses] to class. (J.A.S.: "Why?") Because I have nothing to give to the teachers, and they have nothing to give to me. Besides, half the time I'm stoned.
>
> (age 17)

Our friends are the keys to the fun we hope to have whether it's with them or at their expense. Stabbing each other in the back and kicking each other in the teeth are acceptable paths to a false fun with which we hope to replace the genuine excitement and joy we are missing in life. We've been bruised so many times we are numb, and we don't even feel it any more.

> (age 18, from an underground
> high school newspaper)

In loyalty to their kind, they cannot tolerate our minds.
In loyalty to our kind, we cannot tolerate their
    obstruction.

> ("Crown of Creation," Jefferson Airplane)

Hiding in my room, safe within my room
I touch no one and no one touches me.

> ("I Am a Rock," Simon and Garfunkel)

I would like to preface my own comments about this material with the following observations by Peter Marin; they help to move us quickly from the above quotes to the social and spiritual problems which I feel underlie them.

The problem is not merely that "the system" is brutal and corrupt, nor that war has revealed how savage and cynical a people we are. It is, put simply, that "social reality" seems to have vanished altogether. One finds among the young a profound and befuddled sense of loss—as if they had been betrayed by an entire world.

What is release and space for adults is for them a constant sense of separation—a void in which the self can float and soar but in which one can also drift and fall; and when one falls, it is forever, for there is nothing underneath, no culture, no net of meaning, nobody else.

That is, of course, what we've been talking about

for a century—the existential universe of self-creation. It is a condition of the soul, an absolute loss and yearning for the world. One can become anything—but nothing makes much sense. Adults have managed to evade it, to hesitate on its edges, to cling to one another and to institutions, to beliefs in "the system," to law and order; but now none of that coheres, and the young seem unprotected by it all.

The paradox, of course, is that the dissolution of culture has set us free to create almost anything, but it also deprives us of the abilities to do it: strength, wholeness, and sanity seem to be functions of relationships, and relation, I think, is a function of culture, part of its intricate web of approved connection and experience, a network of persons and moments that simultaneously offer us release and bind us to the lives of others. One "belongs" to and in culture in a way that goes beyond mere politics or participation, for belonging is both simpler and more complex than that; an immersion in the substance of community and tradition, which is itself a net beneath us, a kind of element in which men float, protected. That is, I suppose, what the young have lost. And in the midst of that loss, they seem more beautiful than ever, but maimed, trying against all odds to salvage something from the loss. . . .[1]

I hope it is not difficult to see, in reading these paragraphs, what kind of task I think is in store for religious education, and, at the same time, how unaware and illequipped Jewish teachers are to approach these young people and to help them construct "nets of meaning," the "substance of community and tradition," to suggest to them in their fall that there is something underneath, somebody else. Our inability to do this is symptomatic of our own sickness and paralysis. Perhaps we have not experienced what Marin is describing, or understood how such experience is linked to our political and economic priorities on the national level; we may have been fortunate, or perhaps we have simply "managed to evade it, to hesitate on its edges, to cling to one another and to institutions, to beliefs in the system, to law and order." But we have given the young the affluence and perspective of Koheleth in Ecclesiastes; and in their eyes, we are certainly not busy doing anything that strikes them as more significant than evasion and role-playing in the face of the void.

Young people who see in the "establishment" commuter a man hopelessly torn among competing value systems and group loyalties, sacrificing his spontaneity, his body, his moments of joyful integration, the light in his eyes, the spring in his step, lost in a welter of transactional and performance-oriented relationships, lacking arenas for the expression of deeper affections and the ritualizing of deeper conflicts are prone to reject the whole system, and the elaborate system of ethics and ideologies which rationalize it and lead it to war. Such rejection, depending upon its nature and context, may be a sign of strength and health, not of solipsistic withdrawal. One embraces the perspective from which he can see that few people actually die from pollution or war; rather, they had to "die" before they were able to fight or to pollute. For when we live in a social context which numbs internal life and substitutes transaction for communion, which, in short, creates for millions a living death, anything is possible. To dissent from the societal "death trip" in which we are all caught is to summon resources of health and strength and optimism—resources which psychologist Keniston found in abundance during his study of some early radical experiments like Vietnam Summer. Actually, to live the kind of emotional and ethical life which might flow from such strength and health is to find oneself uncomfortable with so much in the American way of life that one is truly a social deviant.

I am not claiming that all youthful protest is motivated solely by an explicit, rational concern for injustice and the state of current social priorities. Perhaps hardly any of it is. But that is not the point. The point is that even the most irrational and self-defeating of radical experiments and negations often reflect the toll taken by a society such as we have described. We should see in youth revolt an implicit critique and silhouette of our society and the corrupting influence it seems to exercise on human relationships.

Nor am I defending the irrationality of student protest even though I claim that it points to something. Indeed, I believe that a fuller commitment to follow the dictates of reason might lead us to a more effective and adult radicalism which would be operative long after the fires of adolescent trauma had burned themselves out. If there were a mature example of reasoned radicalism, the young might not have to define themselves through such bizarre and generation-centered deviance. Their grasp at a life worth affirming might be less spastic.

If the adolescent's cognitive, emotional, and physical development exposes him to a questioning of a social structure which seems inhospitable to his growth, it also exposes him to deeper questions about what in life *transcends* the existing order. The unpleasant discoveries about society we've been describing come to the young at that stage of life in which fidelity, idealism, and the experience of meaningful commitments are most needed. If the football team and the sorority will not provide arenas in which these satisfactions can be experienced, youth will look elsewhere, increasingly beyond the pale of what is conventional. For theirs is the search for the capacity to "mean" something in an ultimate sense, a capacity which involves Erikson's intersection of self and history. Ours is not a time in which such an intersection is easily brought about, for young people "see through" most of the going traditions, modes, and institutions. Why shouldn't they? We have taught them to.

We have shaken the sanctity of the conventional Meanings and commitments by demonstrating their rootedness in psychic need. We have uncovered the correspondence between the individual's intrapsychic processes and his selective perceptions of "outer" reality, and suggested that since commitments in the "outer" world are energized by needs in the "inner," principled assertion is suspect. The ensuing relativism and skepticism with which we teach the young to encounter systems of Meaning that once guided our own upbringing can lead them to a paralysis which gripped the early existentialists, but which I believe is being experienced by large numbers of suburban youth for the first time today. It is a search for "the courage to be"—and Paul Tillich, who coined the phrase, would prefer to see it as at least as much a religious problem as one for the psychoanalyst.

Unfortunately, the young have been deprived of believable myths, of arenas and occasions for the engagement of passion, celebration of fantasy, expression of eros. Having suffered from this social and spiritual vacuum, they grant a wide margin of credibility to the search for spirituality and for myth, and reject most of the currently available cultural and religious options as shallow imitations of true community. The task of constructing or discovering new "nets of meaning" lies before them. Nothing in the formal education they have received, or in the suburban lives they have been asked to lead, equips them for this task. The need is felt anew for a valued affirmation of life which, however much it employs rigor and reason, nevertheless goes deeper than the scholar's tentativeness and skepticism. The need is for an existential outreach, a leap of faith which is the non-rational prerequisite of all rational activity. In this dimension the religious educator asks what happens when the young reach the existential moment, when they lose the nerve to make the leap of faith, and proclaim themselves unconvinced by ours and what it has to offer (they wear "shades" to class); or when, having made that leap, they opt not for the centrality of social responsibility and suburban life, but for a larger dose of fantasy, celebration, dialogue, and myth in their lives than we have in ours.

In this sketch of youthful discontent I have attempted to remain sympathetic to the suburban Jewish young without glorifying them. To say that their alienation may bear signs of health and be constructive is not, I hope, to deny that when one leaves the social fold he is playing with fire. In the absence of a viable social context which one can trust, spirals of ecstasy alternate with spirals of despair, and it is the rare individual who can survive indefinitely without a sense of history and communal support. But at least one knows he is alive, and struggling with the basics of living; and that in itself is more than one can find when he looks into the eyes of most of his "teachers."

From their forays into the unknown the young bring back considerable wisdom; at times one feels that at seventeen they are as sad and as wise as their parents. They are not too often happy in their vaunted life-styles, though I would suggest that some are deriving more satisfaction and intimacy from communes than they did from that peculiar living arrangement known as the suburban nuclear family.

Any evaluation of youth turmoil must make us aware of what is legitimate and potentially fruitful in this anguish, what is subtle and beautiful in the search they pursue in a spiritually and morally bankrupt society. From the anguish of the adolescent we learn the general principle that the collective consciousness of the school or peer group or community or nation can no more remain starved for shared fantasy and myth than can the individual psyche remain starved for love and commitment and faith and home. It might be dangerously wrong to "settle down" and "adjust" to a grievous lack of these things.

Jewish Education

It is not only in the fascination of some young people with Hasidic and Kabbalic sources that Judaism may find itself a crucial contributor to their lives. It has often occurred to me that not only the prophetic and the mystic, but even the more rabbinic and normative streams of Jewish tradition would concur with the young in their evaluation of our social priorities and religious decay. Of course it is equally clear that Jewish tradition would not go all the way with the young on their forays after universal truth; it would suggest that spiritual flight had best take communal (not self-indulgent) routes, that the aesthetics of the righteous deed and the soft answer should take precedence over the aesthetics of sensual gratification. It would deride the aesthetic hedonism of the bauble-and-bead stores patronized by so many "hip" young people, and it would resist the stylistic radicalism of those who follow radical communities in the same way their predecessors followed the status elites of an earlier era. It would suggest that one cannot be sloppy about the alternatives he would affirm as he opposes current situations (see "The Case for Religious Radicalism" in this volume). The point, I believe, is that Jewish tradition would share youth's critique without supporting everything kids have done (or been duped into doing) as a result of that critique. It offers examples of constructive alternatives—alternatives which range as far afield as the mystic and the ecstatic, but alternatives that substitute community for conventionality, and knowledge for nihilism.

What is equally clear, of course, is that the organized American Jewish community—including most of its rabbis and educators—is offering no real help whatsoever to those young people struggling along the frontiers of self-fulfillment I have tried to sketch. In part, this is because the young people I am describing are hardly visible to Jewish educators; they sit behind dutiful masks in class, or do not enroll at all, abandoning what they can see of Jewish life with a mild shrug. In the perspective of a radical critique which links the hollowness of daily suburban life to the elaborate synagogues, one can only sympathize with the girl in my Westport confirmation class who said somewhat wistfully, "My life is too rich and beautiful for Judaism." What is sad is that the things which do make her life "rich and beautiful" are so meager and threadbare in comparison to the riches of Jewishness; yet they are grasped and held so strongly because they are personal and real, something Judaism is not.

It will not do to "argue" with her. These are not matters subject to influence by classroom debate. The Jewish school (which is to say the teachers in it and the kind of trusting atmosphere they have managed to radiate) would have to be a place where she felt supported enough and strong enough to examine the limits of her current "alternatives," and to encounter the power of Jewishness. Yet how can such a Jewish school exist if we have copied the modern public schools both in our architecture and in our administrations, let alone in our teaching styles? What is true of them is true of the Jewish school; they have become, according to Peter Marin,

> stiff, unyielding microcosmic versions of a world that has already disappeared for the young. Their real outrage is their systematic corruption of the relations among persons; their corrosive role-playing and demand systems are so extensive, so profound, that nothing really human shows through—and when it does, it appears only as frustration, exhaustion, anger.[2]

Where, one might ask, is the Jewish teacher, the beloved teacher whom we are commanded to create for ourselves in another, toward whom we gravitate because he radiates enthusiasm and acquires through his commitment a natural authority which need not be buttressed by institutional regulations? One begins to understand what is lacking most sorely in religious education when he rediscovers the Jewish student-teacher relationship, keeping in mind Buber's belief that

> The relation in education is one of pure dialogue . . . Trust, trust in the world, because this human being exists, that is the most inward achievement of the relationship in education. Because this human being exists, meaninglessness, however hard-pressed you are by it, cannot be the real truth. Of course the teacher cannot be continually concerned with the child, nor ought he to be. But if he has really gathered the child into his life, then that subterranean dialogic, the steady potential presence of the one to the other, is established and endures.[3]

One need not have such a teacher to learn matters of fact, especially when we can presume on the part of the student a desire to learn the knowledge to be presented. In matters of commitment, however, matters involving that subtle and fragile encounter between the growing self and the tradition, a sensitive mediator and guide is necessary. Jewish education for the young is not to be confused with the academic scholarship of Judaica professors anxious to maintain their university credentials. Rather, it is a more total and affective fusion—one in which rigor and detachment are at times indispensable, but never sufficient.

The irony is that our children increasingly know this already. Conscious, articulate dissatisfaction with public high school education is widespread among Jewish high school students. Jewish education misses its unique opportunity to meet the searching young with both the style and content of its own modes of learning. It can offer the riches of a tradition in which men are not afraid to utter words which make them tremble, in which precious moments and communal settings are cultivated and nurtured, and in which there are such rich and colorful ways of elevating youth's alienation to the level of spiritual commitment and prophetic dissent. That such a tradition as the Jewish people's should fail to support and elicit potential parallels among the suburban young would cause outrage if its prostitution to the status quo were not by now such a tired old story.

Jewish education for these young people will have to build its own supportive community of action and shared ritual, because the existing organized Jewish community is little more than a collection of mimeograph machines and pooled nostalgia. The Jewish school must be not a set of classrooms but a tentative community which provides hints of viable cultural, spiritual, and interpersonal alternatives to the emptiness of students' current pressured, cram-packed, instrumental, goal-oriented, and fragmented lives. In a world which stimulates impulse-buying and sensual gratification as supreme values, a world which lures individuals into an economic system based upon false and fabricated scarcities, a world which compartmentalizes religious, symbolic, and non-utilitarian actions and relationships and confines them to Sunday morning, a world whose concepts of space and time wreak havoc upon soul and sacred moments, to engage in Jewish education may be to "corrupt the young," for such education would surely support a measure of their alienation from the suburban cultural nets we've described. Such Jewish education will surely not bring the young to membership in empty suburban temples, which makes me wonder how it could possibly have the support of professional rabbis and synagogue leaders.

Yet it is precisely the need for a communal context which serves as an *alternative* to the youngster's school and home life which explains why Jewish education has been moderately successful in the summer camps, to some extent in Israel, and through the *havurot,* as well as in those more imaginative schools which have action projects, frequent *Shabbat* retreats, and an atmosphere which makes the school area itself a place where young people actually want to "hang around." (Young people usually do not trust themselves to areas surrounded by cinder blocks, waxed tiles, and fluorescent lights; the use of these materials in the building of Jewish schools shows for whom they are really built and what philosophies of education they are meant to support.)

This is not the place to recount in detail the successful attempts at fusing an understanding of the young with a reform of curriculum and methodology, to tell of *Shabbat* retreats which released a virtual flood of previously dammed-up emotional and spiritual needs, to describe the traditionally authentic uses of evocative biblical texts to make a classroom a moral community. Suffice it to say that, against the backdrop of what is best in the tradition, and what is most needed by the suburban Jewish young, there are at least three basic ingredients to Jewish education: 1) a knowledge and powerful personal internalization of Jewishness on the part of the teacher; 2) an openness to dialogic relationship, communal membership, and a willingness to undergo personal change in response to students; and 3) the existence, however furtive and primitive, of a Jewish community (like the summer camp, the *havurah*, the core of the class which went on a successful series of retreats last year) which the young would like to join. Only in these contexts—knowledge, interpersonal sensitivity, and communal action—can Jewish education take place. It *begins* not with the tradition but with eliciting the students' concerns and with nurturing what is best in them, in an effort to establish trust and to learn. Throughout, it must be borne in mind and heart that knowledge in this case is more than academic knowledge; sensitivity is not technique or therapeutic condescension; community is not the school Hanukah assembly or the synagogue board of trustees.

Religious education in our age ought to be, among other things, that arena in which the search for meaningful, human styles of spiritual and communal life is pursued by young and old together—by those young, that is, who can be brought to grant that there may be much of strength and beauty somewhere in an accessible past, and by elders who are willing to admit that for all their wisdom and indulgent perspective they may not be near what they could be. If there *is* strength and beauty in the past, I presume that it will emerge in the personalities, deeds, and messages of those who teach the young, write papers about them, or make claims upon them. Otherwise it is a dead past, a lost past, and the young will have to survive by themselves, to learn it all from scratch on more levels than the average individual can bear.

What is demanded of the older generation (although this will be severely tested by the young before it is believed) is a living spectacle of fulfilled, loving people who radiate a fundamental affirmation about life, not a series of negative cautions about what will happen if stylized patterns are abandoned.

To me the Jewish community in history has represented an arena in which such a joyful passing-on of fundamental affirmations from old to young—and back— was felt. I am suggesting that if the Jewish community is to remain such an arena, it may have to alienate itself from, and be increasingly critical of, the general drift of American society. We will have to learn about the subtle, insidious weakening of our communal fiber which has taken place under the heavy hand of competitive individualism, the demand for efficiency, and the worship of profit. When we face the facts, and come around to the realization that there is precious little in America as she is today which supports meaningful religious communities, we may be surprised to find that our young intuited this critique long ago, and have just about given up waiting for us to arrive. There is still time to hope that if the

American Jewish community truly rejoins the Jewish people and Jewish history it might meet its young people again, and thereby prepare itself to make vital contributions to the American future. From the Jewish community I would like to envision we would hear no automatic sigh of relief when, at age twenty-five, the once-impatient youth settles resignedly into suburbia, temple membership, and the societal "death trip."

Over the past few years increasing numbers of Jewish educators have found that culturally viable Jewish religious communities are not compatible with the life of the American urban or suburban nuclear family; in their own lives they feel the weight of American life dissolving cultures and fragmenting identities. They realistically doubt their personal capacity to effect the kind of radical change in social priorities which would be needed to make meaningful living possible again. And so the beginning of the great exodus to Israel is now being monitored across the land. Left behind are the suburban Jewish young, without roots and memories, caught in a limbo of alienation from America, which they see as a kind of cosmic stage, but not as a supportive culture, and of estrangement from the historical journey of their people. They are left to join the long line of Jewish intellectuals and artists who tried to overcome homelessness and alienation through creativity, radical activity, and revolution, men who changed the course of Western history through commercialism and communism, psychoanalysis and relativity, while thrashing unknowingly in the chains of their own Jewish enslavement and estrangement. Unless we would move them to Israel, we will have to face the fact that we cannot create for them a viable Jewish community in America without a severe critique of our current economic and cultural situation.

In the past, of course, the Jew's alienation was his own problem. But for once it is not only the Jewish youth in America who finds himself bereft of viable culture, and homeless. For perhaps the first time in history, he is joined by large numbers of his non-Jewish peers, including both the white Anglo-Saxon Protestant and the black. A strong Jewish prophecy will ring not only in Jewish, but also in American ears.

In this sense, the duty of Jewish education to America is to attempt to restore the moral and prophetic dimension to efforts at social change, to provide a responsible and constructive militancy, not a substitute for militancy. It should aid in the creation of the supportive, healthy communal base from which radicalism emerges not as deviance but as an expression of mainstream prophecy on the part of the community. That kind of radical Jewish community—radical because to preserve its Jewishness it challenges American economic and political arrangements—has begun to take feeble root in the thin and shifting soil on the margins of the American Jewish community. It affirms Jewishness and the viability of the resources of the tradition. Its reading of the tradition and of the Jew's potential role in history is becoming increasingly sophisticated, and hopefully that reading will compete with the conventions of the more "normative," seminary- and organization-based community for the minds and hearts of the suburban Jewish young. Its insight is that Jewish commitment is not compatible with what America is becoming. Its hope is that by its meaningful survival the Jewish community in America may help to heal this incompatibility even as, through Jewish education, it heals the broken spirits among youth who are the chief and saddest victims of the split.

NOTES

1. Peter Marin, "Children of the Apocalypse," *Saturday Review*, Sept. 19, 1970, p. 72.
2. *Ibid.*, p. 73.
3. Martin Buber, *Between Man and Man*, New York: Macmillan, 1965, p. 98.

Raphael Arzt is a rabbi and director of a Jewish summer camp called Ramah. The setting has been of increasing importance in the evolving of Jewish education because it provides a unique opportunity for presenting Jewishness as an experiential totality rather than as a primarily academic enterprise. In camps like Ramah, educators are forced to understand and interpret Judaism in terms of life-style, everyday situations, and social ethics. Through this effort, in which Rabbi Arzt has been an articulate participant, many young Jews have been initiated into a viable Jewish commitment during formative years.

In this important interview, Rabbi Arzt addresses the perplexing category of Jewish law as a framework through which the dimensions of religious life-style and social ethics may be approached. In a relativized society, such law is not an absolute but rather an existential internalization of an imperative, the accepting upon oneself of the duty of responsiveness to an evolving set of norms and disciplines. Tradition is seen as a rich resource of experience, and law as a way our aspirations and sentiments will be translated into a workable reality.

Rabbi Arzt was ordained by the Jewish Theological Seminary of America. Last year he was in Israel completing a thesis on Jewish education for his doctorate at Columbia University.

Imperative and Conscience
in Jewish Law*

an interview with RAPHAEL ARZT

Q: *Since, today, Judaism has taken on so many aspects —social action, prayer, organic community—to what extent do you find this involvement in a legal tradition an exciting or vital part of Judaism?*

A: First let us understand that law connotes an imperative. Whether imposed by a social system or imposed upon oneself, law is not an option; it is an imperative. Jewish law has historically permeated every area of life: civil, ritual, familial, private, and communal. If you ask: does the law have a central role in light of areas like social action or worship, the answer is that the theology of law would dominate these areas. Viewing law as a theology, you wouldn't decide to become involved in a dimension

---

* This selection originally appeared in *Response*, Vol. I, No. 1, Summer 1967.

like social action because you like it, or it's good as a personal option. You would feel it as an imperative—I must get involved in this, since this is the way I'm commanded (without going into the nature of divine command now). At one time, the theology of law, which I am defining as the need for imperatives, and the sociology of law, which was the implementation of imperatives in specific social circumstances (communities), were closely intertwined—were one and the same thing. One had to be involved, in his community, in an agency to allow him to implement the social goals of helping the underprivileged. He had to, since the community and tradition demanded it.

Today, we have a bifurcation. The sociological and theological are torn apart. We don't have a *Jewish* sociology. We have ghettos, but no real Jewish sociology. We have a repository of all kinds of law, without social agencies to implement it. This is why we get stagnation—no sense of divine imperatives and no social agencies to implement them.

Q: *Suppose we apply this situation to ritual. Don't we have to examine the forms of our ritual to see if they themselves or their traditional meanings have relevance in our society? Might we not have adopted the forms of a past sociology, devoid of contemporary meaning? For example, at Camp Ramah it is a norm of the camp to observe* kashrut. *Therefore no one asks crucial questions about these laws of dietary ritual. However, on return to the city, the individual finds himself in a society in which* kashrut *is not a norm and must ask himself: what is the value of this ritual for me? This seems parallel to the change we were speaking of in Judaism. The "traditional" [or camp] sociology, which gave meaning to a ritual, disappears; the individual is left with a form which he must now examine for himself.*

A: This problem is a new one for Judaism. It is grounded in the fact that the fundamental basis of any commitment today, in my opinion, must be an existential one. I am using existential in a descriptive sense: I must decide what is meaningful and what is not. For example, even if I were to take the full Jewish legal system upon myself as my life pattern, it is first as a decision of mine; and then I take it on myself as an obligation. I commit myself to Jewish law rather than *it* committing *me* simply as a norm of the society. Therefore, any value I commit myself to will be a value that I choose, insofar as I'm aware that choices are involved. Living in an American middle-class suburban community, I'm living out all kinds of values that I'm not aware of. But, in those areas of which I am aware—where decision-making is involved—such as when I go out to a restaurant and decide I will eat fish on non-kosher dishes, it is clear that I am making a decision, whether I like it or not.

Q: *This is a new Judaism then . . .*

A: It's not only Judaism. It's the characteristic of contemporary Western man. Once you have the breakdown of the Platonic idea of ideals, of absolutes (first for an intellectual class, and now in general) and life is defined by a process of hypothetical thinking, testing, and evaluating, once you've broken down your ideals and have tentativeness, process, and relativism in operation, any kind of life you're going to lead is going to be a choice-life and not a sociologically determined life. Therefore, the problem a person has with *kashrut* is a problem of choice. The elements that go into making that choice are (a) to what extent does the person have a simple concern for his Jewishness (today you even have a choice to be or not be concerned with your Jewishness), and (b) if I choose to be concerned (and only then), by what set of criteria will I make decisions about the items of my Jewishness. Therefore, one person may say: I choose to be kosher on the identity basis. In other words, I'm identifying with my Jewishness through observing *kashrut*. I know I eat three times a day and this is a very powerful identity symbol. Every time I walk into Chock Full o' Nuts and look at that menu and know I can't order a hamburger, but have to get a cheese sandwich instead, that has an identity link—if I want to identify. It's an option, a piece of repertoire that's available to me. So, one criterion is identification.

Another is the criterion of personal holiness. It would read something like this: I want to convert my table into an altar before God; every time I partake of a piece of food, I want to be reminded of my relationship to God, of His generosity, of the difference between man and animal. That would be a holiness criterion. Another person would use both—what I call a spectrum or conspectus rationale. Still, he is selecting the criteria. He's making the decisions, selecting the life-style. He may also choose to commit himself to the Law in its totality because he feels that only in that way can he keep Judaism from disappearing.

Q: *Could we explore this idea of holiness?*

A: The holiness concept is a very difficult idea. *Kedusha* (holiness) is what I would call an open-ended concept. My own definition would state that *kedusha* is reached in many areas of human experience when what is ultimately significant is approached. When you reach, or approach, the highest ideal level of interpersonal relationships, you are at a moment of *kedusha.* Or take the case of the dietary system, *kashrut.* If at the moment that you make a decision for *kashrut* it evolves the fullest range of meaning possible, be it at a meal or whatever, and it brings in its wake a whole enriched range of reflections, associations, meditations, feelings, and cues for further action, then that is a moment of *kedusha,* because the symbol has evoked its maximum.

Q: *To what extent is your own observance a mixture of the identity principle and this matter of holiness?*

A: Being a professional Jew, I will never know what I would be like if I weren't a professional. Let us bear that in mind. But as well as I can understand, the major part of my life was as a sociological Jew—an identity-tied Jew. I have continued basic patterns learned in my childhood, through my home and education. After some time, I became reflective about those patterns. That means that as I reflected upon my sociological base, I began to expand the existential quality of it and to try to evoke deeper meaning in my religious experience. I'm very ready to say that there are certain things I do that are really very shallow in terms of why I do them—they're sociological. But that sociology is always there. That is, I have the open-ended sense that I can change that sociology into higher levels of perception if I so will it. I'll give you an example: Once, I prayed sociologically. I used to sit in the last row of the synagogue and talk to my friends. That could be nothing but a sociological enterprise. I think I studied Judaically in high school, and maybe even in the seminary, on a sociological basis. After coming under the influence of some of the thought of Rabbi Zalman Schachter, I began to see the need not only to fulfill the *mitzvah* (the commandment) but the *hiddur mitzvah,* the personal enhancement of the commandment. I started with the sociological base, the given, and then tried to pull meanings out of it: meanings, some of which were highly personal and private, some of which were profound, and some of which were simple (but meaningful to me). It is that aspect of what I tried to do to the sociology that I call the enhancement of commandment—the enhancement being the bringing of my personality to bear on the given, an accommodation of the given to me—which produced my Jewish life-style and whatever quality I might have to my religious life.

So now, when I go to synagogue I generally know that I have to do something to convert that into a meaningful experience. If I don't do anything, nothing's going to happen. The rabbi's not going to help me; the *hazan* is not going to help me, and my wife certainly isn't going to help me. So one of the things I do as a safeguard is to always sit on the end of a row, the last seat, because when I pray I want to get apart from certain aspects of the service and be by myself while still being part of the community itself. That physical act is a self-conscious act. This self-consciousness was developed by Schachter into the idea of repertoire of responses: the realization that there are a variety of responses that one can give religiously, and that you don't have to fall into a given mold.

Q: *This infusing of the given with meaning seems to presuppose creativity and self-consciousness on the part of the observer. Does this mean that only an elite will be able to observe Judaism meaningfully?*

A: When you are talking about a full religious expression, you are talking about an open elite. That is an elite which anyone, given basic intellectual and emotional health, can move into as a function of his training, sensitivity, etc. Each person, given the basic tools, will decide how to operate with those tools.

Q: *Then, in personal observance, to what is the individual responsible?*

A: I think he's responsible to his own sense of integrity, integrity meaning his relationship to his overall articulated commitments. For example, the person says: "I am committed to the concept of regular worship as broadly outlined in the tradition." He therefore sees the good that accrues in setting aside regular periods for worship. He is then responsible to concretize that commitment. Whether he does it once a day, once a week, or three times a week depends on his expanding need. If he says: "I want to worship Jewishly," and the Jewish law calls for prayer three times a day, that is what he wants his mode of worship to be. Otherwise, he feels the tension between what he professes and what he is.

Q: *You have stated that the tradition provides a base from which the individual can grow and expand. Why wouldn't any other jumping-off place do?*

A: The tradition is in this case instrumental. That is

the traditional idea also. That is the meaning of the whole idea of there being a point in history when you will not need laws and rituals, but every man will know what to do—that is, the ultimate vision. What you're groping toward in your question is the idea that without the tradition, I would work with my own innards and develop a spiritual life. I seriously doubt it. Knowing myself, knowing my problematic response to the tradition, even those elements of the tradition which are meaningful to me, and knowing that my responses differ depending on my mood, I have grave doubts that I would have the emotional stability to build a coherent, transmittable spiritual life—on my own—which I think I can now build with the given of the tradition as the point of departure.

Q: *But don't you have to take into account to whom it's transmitted? Is Judaism "a coherent, transmittable, spiritual life" suitable for everyone?*

A: I think that there are within Judaism so many streams that a person who is religiously interested can find one that suits him. There is a strong social concern stream, a strong normative-mystical stream, and a strong communal stream. He can always find something of meaning in his Jewish associations. You and I will be members of the same synagogue; you will study at the time when you should be praying; and I'll be praying like mad. Why? Because temperamentally and intellectually you're more suited to one thing than another.

Q: *What happens when a ritual no longer holds significance for any major segment of the community? Shall we still retain it?*

A: Let me say this: if the ritual does not take on new significance, it will wither and die. Still, it will not die really, because it will be recorded in the tradition and always will have the possibility of being revived again. I think you see a reawakening of the social action and ethical concerns today. Previously, there had been more of a movement toward identity, keeping the Jewish people together.

Q: *Since your approach to ritual has been individual, how do you react to the current desire for central direction in Jewish law?*

A: No central group can really tell me how to act religiously. It may be easier taking instructions, but I'm stating an existential fact. Even if a group met and produced the profoundest statement in the world, just the fact that it produced it is not going to make me act that way.

What the center can do is bring coherence into a very incoherent picture, at this point. If the last Jewish legal codification was Karo's, then we need a new codification. But it must be a codification in contemporary terms, as all the codifications have been in their own context. I'd imagine the new codification would be a statement of the fundamental Jewish values, then a listing of how those values were concretized, historically, in law. But in suburbia, with people living up to ten miles from the synagogue, it would make no sense to say that the historical "listing" of not riding should be one of the prime concretizations of the observance of the Sabbath. I'd rather build a list of positive elements that would concretize a contemporary Sabbath observance. In general, the next step in the codification would be, on the basis of a sociological analysis today, to indicate how best these fundamental Jewish values can be concretized in terms of the Jewish community today. Then I might want to add a list of recommended enrichments, such as not riding.

In summary then, we need a reworking of the rationale of the legal system, an identification of the key values, a sharpening of what the key pillars are, and a recommended positive program. The rest is up to the responding, choosing, individual Jew.

Part Two

Religious Imagination

David G. Roskies is a significant and unique voice in the youth community, a fact which is partially explained by his background. He was born in Montreal in 1948. A graduate of the Jewish People's School, he continued his study of Judaism at Brandeis University, where he is now pursuing a doctorate. He is literary editor of Yugntruf, an international Yiddish youth quarterly. He is a member of Havurat Shalom, contemplating offering a course there in Eastern European Jewish culture.

Because of this training and knowledge, David is among the few who can transcend sentimentalism in dealing with the millennium of Jewish life in Eastern Europe. He is special in being able to experiment with connections and syntheses between cultural secularism and current religious search.

In this essay David explores the potential relationship between a medium and a civilization, that is, between film and Judaism. Excited by the possibilities film holds for the renewing and revivifying of Judaism, he outlines how the process of realizing Jewish symbols cinematically might be undertaken. He presents also the depth and quality of knowledge of the Jewish past a film maker would have to possess to effect such translations.

The Celluloid Jew[*]

by DAVID G. ROSKIES

[*for H.S.*]

The film begins quietly, with a gentle rhythm. The faint
sounds of communal prayer grow louder as the camera
pans over the village market and focuses its lens on an im-
posing wooden structure, a combination pagoda and
blockhouse. Except for the church, it is the highest building in the *shtetl*. As the camera moves in, past the ante-
room known as the *polish*, the viewer meets the intricate,
cluttered design of the interior, all in wood. A motley
group of Jews are engaged in morning prayer. They are
wearing the traditional Eastern European garb, in various
stages of disrepair. None of the men can be recognized as
world-renowned actors uncomfortably disguised as Orthodox Jews. All the faces are anonymous. The prayer is

* This selection originally appeared in *Response*, Vol. IV, No. 1, Spring
1970.

not marked by ecstatic behavior. Most of those present are in a hurry to open up shop. In a side room, a group of elderly Jews can be seen studying out loud as they rock back and forth, apparently oblivious of the service. The voices converge into a mild confusion of sounds: low- and high-pitched, hoarse and melodic, fervent and indifferent. The audience is not expected to recognize the prayers or the particular tractate being studied. Moreover, there are no subtitles at all in the film, even during the dialogue. The actors speak Yiddish, in a dialect peculiar to the region being depicted. Their speech is irrelevant, however, for this is a film about irrational forces that negate the ordered universe of the word. The Jews conduct their lives as usual, arguing and counter-arguing, channeling their wit and aggression into the word, searching for ways to reduce pandemonium to rational size. In vain. There are no options open. This is not a Talmudic tractate. Their world is about to be disrupted by irrational violence: predictable, endemic and short-lived.

The sounds move into the market which is only beginning to show signs of life. The cries of the first vegetable vendors, the curses of the half-drowsing beggars. Ragged children off to *kheyder* (school). To the cinematic eye, the scene recalls not *Fiddler on the Roof,* but *The World of Apu,* with its squalor and its starkness. Perhaps it shocks those for whom the *shtetl* is epitomized by the colorful array of costumes, the bottle dance and the songs in the wedding sequence of that Broadway production of the Sholem Aleichem classic; or to stay in the same medium, by an even briefer wedding scene in the American film version of an American Jewish novel on the life of a famous Eastern European Jew named Mendl Beyles.

Slowly, imperceptibly, the rhythm of the film changes. The shots become disjointed. New characters are introduced. A wandering preacher delivering hellfire sermons in the church. The appearance of strange *goyim* in town, their secretiveness. Rumors and counter-rumors. With an ostensibly detached eye the lens watches it happen, watches the Jews watching it happen. Finally, the tension snaps and violence erupts: theft, murder, rape. The nameless Jews who were going about their business only minutes before are now flung into a whirlpool of violence. The metaphors of past experience burst into a red vacuum. Surely this is not the *Akeyda,* the sacrifice on Mount Moriah? It isn't even an auto-da-fé. Merely a gang of drunken *goyim* destroying and defiling. All that remains are the feathers on the muddy streets. The pogromists always tear open the stolen bedding and strew it all over town. To cover up the blood? As a ritual of completion?

The viewer's understanding of the film will depend on his familiarity with the Jewish culture of Eastern Europe. He who is linguistically prepared will experience the shock of the pogrom through the rape of language. In the time span of the film, he will pass from the sanctified sounds of the Hebrew-Aramaic, to the vibrant ring of the market vernacular, to the brutal cries of a Ukrainian dialect. He who is knowledgeable in Jewish history will sense the irony of the Chosen People concept, so central to the liturgy, being turned on its head by the reality of Jewish vulnerability. The untutored viewer will partake of a purely visual experience—the dynamic of violence that tears apart a self-contained mini-world, oblivious to the outside. Perhaps he will draw implications from more recent events in history.

The first obstacle in creating a Jewish film idiom, then, is ignorance. Without a knowledge of the myriad of past associations that make up Jewish culture, there can be no Jewish art of the present. Contemporary Jewish symbols are meaningless if uprooted from the frame of reference of past experience. Jewish art that ignores its past will never transcend the level of documentary. Film is the medium that can bridge the gap between the Jewish symbol and its consumer audience. Film, above all else, can familiarize a public of millions upon millions of people with otherwise unknown regions and cultural patterns. The cinematic public can learn to recognize Maggidim as easily as it does Samurai, or to know the inner workings of the court of Menaham Mendl of Kotsk as well as it knows the details of the Czarist court in Ivan the Terrible's time. The public has assimilated enough Christian symbolism to recognize a beggar's feast in Luis Bunuel's *Viridiana* as a grotesque parody of the Last Supper. It is a public that can appreciate the multitude of allusions to Christian myth in the films of Ingmar Bergman. Bunuel and Bergman have the advantage of working with symbols that have dominated the Western mind for over a thousand years. They can go ahead devising variations, modern applications and perversions. The Jewish *cinéaste* cannot assume such prior knowledge.

Indeed, where will his own pool of visual symbols, metaphors and associations derive from? He has the Bible. That's always good for a start. But how will that help him film the life of Eastern European Jewry, for example? His search will lead him to the language and literature of Yiddish speaking Jews. He will discover a world in which Tevye can look up at the trees and compare their shadows to the endlessness of *goles*, of dispersion; or Agnon's semi-mythical world in which snow on a Saturday night is compared to the feathers on angels' wings spread out to honor Israel.

In the mind of the Jew, past and present were one and indivisible. The biblical promise was not a metaphor but an immediacy. One Jew brags to another about owning a book which he considers rare. Retorts the other: "Is there only one red cow in the world?" The reference is to the sin

offering described in Numbers 19:2. Esau, in the folk imagination, became synonymous with a *goy,* especially a
muscular one. When someone was rich, he was "as rich as
Korah," referring to the Talmudic legend about the
wealthy Levite Korah. For a futile activity, Jews said:
"carrying straw to Egypt." In the ritual of introducing the
three-year-old *kheyder-yingl* to Bible study, one of his
contemporaries, assuming the role of the *bentsher,* said:
"Bow your little head and I shall bless you: May you have
a wife with twelve locks and may each lock possess the
sanctity of the tribes."

Past and present met and coalesced not only in the language but also in the life of the *shtetl* Jew—where but in
the cemetery, the good place, as it is called in Yiddish. The
beys-oylem (literally, house of the eternal) was a focal
point of the *shtetl,* crowded with graves and visited with
regularity. In times of stress one came to cry one's heart
out at the parental tombs. The practice is appropriately
called *raysn kvorim,* tearing graves. Before Jews emigrated from their towns, they visited these graves to take
leave of the dead. In the film version of Ansky's *The
Dybbuk* (Poland, 1938), gravestones and cemeteries
served as leitmotifs in the plot. The tomb of a married
couple cut down by the Cossacks during their wedding
ceremony now stood in the market place at the very spot
of their murder. Leah, the heroine of the film, visited her
lover's grave and a "lap dissolve" turned the gravestone
into a cradle. The Miropolyer Rebbe, who was called upon
to exorcise the *dybbuk,* sent his attendant to the graveyard
to call Khonon's father to a trial. The symbolist writer Der
Nister, one of the Soviet Yiddish writers purged by Stalin,
entitled his last story written in that genre "Unter a Ployt,"
beyond a fence, the place where outcasts were buried.
What better metaphor for a writer who was stifled into
compliance and who renounced his aesthetic personality.
Or for Lamed Shapiro, the master of the Yiddish short

story, for whom the cemetery with its peace and solitude became the perfect foil for the turmoil and misery of the living Jewish community.

In order to reinterpret the life of the Eastern European Jew, as did Ansky, Der Nister, Shapiro and virtually every modern Yiddish writer, the Jewish film maker will have to at least be familiar with the bare outlines of that world, its concerns and its myths. The cemetery, as suggested, concentrated many of these beliefs and practices into one plot of land. Clearly, another such place was the *shul;* the synagogue, not only as a place of worship but a place for the redress of grievances, where social outcasts could be imprisoned (in the *polish*); a place of study and a refuge for the poor and wandering. The wooden synagogue with its interior design perfected through centuries by artists who had no other outlet for artistic expression.

Judaism was and remains a primarily verbal civilization. The second task of the Jewish film maker is to translate the verbal into visual terms. Suppose he decided to make a film about one of the greatest Jewish personalities of all times, Rabbi Nahman of Bratzlav. One approach could be to portray him as a bohemian poet, a man who refused to be straight-jacketed by tradition. He could film his poetic visions. Scene: Rabbi Nahman walking through a thick forest (which means nothing unless one knows that all mysteries occur in forests, unless one knows the fear and fascination Jews had of the forest). Nahman sees a young man asleep under a tree and thinks up the story of the lost princess and the three futile attempts of the King's messenger to find her. Suppose the film succeeded in evoking the mystery of the forest and the fantasy of the tale. Could it possibly hint at the fact that the princess represented the *Shechina*, the Divine Presence, and that the messenger was the people of Israel?

Another approach could be making the film into an adventure story, portraying Reb Nahman's hair-raising voyage to the Holy Land in 1798. It would include the scene on board ship in which he is suspected of being a spy for the French (Napoleon must have been hard pressed to employ a Yiddish speaking, bearded spy!), as well as Reb Nahman's suspenseful encounter with a huge Turk who was out to kill him. But how could the director suggest the reasons for Nahman's journey, the role of *Eretz Yisrael* in the mind of the Eastern European Jew?

A third possibility would be to film the last year of Nahman's life, the fire in Bratzlav, his moving to Umman and his run-in with the *Maskilim* (enlightened Jews) of that town. The film could be made into a statement about the man of faith vs. the arrogant non-believer. But how could the film explain that Nahman went to Umman to redeem the souls of the Jews killed in a pogrom some thirty years earlier and never properly buried? Or could the film suggest the tensions working in Nahman's mind as he spoke to the heretics; was he redeeming the sparks, was he trying to prove that a pious Jew like himself could also be versed in philosophy and rational science? How much of that could come across on film?

The task is not impossible. There are precedents to study, albeit few in number, but significant nonetheless. One film, already mentioned, stands out as a model of creative Jewish cinema. *The Dybbuk* was shot with a limited budget over thirty years ago by a dedicated group of Yiddish actors and cultural activists. No effort was spared to present an authentic picture of Jewish life in the nineteenth century. The film was shot on location in the Polish town of Kuzmir. In order to insure accurate historical detail, Professor Meir Balaban, later to be murdered by the Nazis, was asked to serve as adviser. By strange coincidence, the director hired was a non-Jew who pioneered the Polish talkies. Just as the famous Habima version of the play was directed by the Armenian Vakhtangov, so the film was directed by Michal Waszynski, who probably knew no Yiddish.

The Dybbuk is a love story of Khonon, a young mystic,

and Leah, a romantically inclined girl, who are caught up in a tragedy of fate and ambition. To date, it is still the most authentic depiction of a Hasidic milieu on film. Abraham Morevsky's interpretation of the Miropolyer Rebbe remains an artistic tour de force.

Like the imaginary film described at the outset, *The Dybbuk* weaves its story around literary allusions as well as visual effects. It too opens in a *shul,* this time during a *Sukkot* service, and the Hasidim are seen engaged in the Hoshana ritual. As the film progresses, the antithetical powers of darkness suggest themselves in the frantic Kabbalistic practice of the young student. These powers are held in check temporarily by the recitation of the Song of Songs which mutes the passion of the hero into a traditional, acceptable idiom. Again, only the initiated viewer will benefit thereof.

The film introduces a whole array of traditional *shtetl* figures: the wagon driver, the matchmaker, the water carrier and, most important, the mysterious messenger. The latter appears throughout Jewish literature in various guises: as Der Geyer (the one who walks) or as Elijah the Prophet. In *The Dybbuk,* he fades in and out of the landscape and acts both as the harbinger of fate and as a moral guide. Fate, in the Jewish concept, is equivocal. It can be appealed by proper moral conduct. Unfortunately, the ambition of Leah's father blinds him to the dangers of toying with fate and his error causes the ruin of both lovers.

To a non-Jewish critic, *The Dybbuk* is "medieval in its spirituality, dimly historical in its Jewishness." To the knowledgeable Jewish viewer, the film offers a fascinating spectrum of an intense way of life saturated with detail and with allusions to tradition.

It is possible, therefore, to transpose one moment in the life of the *shtetl* onto film. There is a literary tradition to fall back upon. But what of the more recent history of the Jew? What of the *gotterdammerung* of Ashkenazic

Jewry? While the pogrom was an isolated occurrence in time and place, the holocaust is a timeless event not bound by town or country. How to apply time-bound metaphors to such an eventless event? What is wanted are metaphors that hint above them—metaphors that express their own inadequacy. Such is the language of film.

The Pawnbroker has come closest to this problem, though its means are somewhat too sensational. *The Pawnbroker* evokes the unreality of the Destruction by remaining scrupulously realistic. Suburbia. Harlem. Apartment complex. A New York park. And the flashbacks. The universe is mad. Thus each object, no matter how mundane, is itself and its antithesis. A ring is not a symbol of matrimony. It is the stripping of identity before the final act. A woman's breasts do not represent the maternal instinct, but rather the human body as a commodity for inhuman consumption. A train is not a utilitarian invention. It transports its human cargo from Purgatory into the Inferno. Here realism is ineffectual, for realism is that which simplifies by virtue of being logical or systematizes by virtue of being useful. No context to contain the event. No frame of reference. Is the metaphor a six-digit number tatooed on Nazerman's arm? Is it his symbolic crucifixion? Is the metaphor chaos? Is it silence?

The Jewish film maker must take a vow of humility before he adjusts his camera lens to shoot the first frame. He is assuming a tremendous responsibility, though it is not fashionable to speak of art in moral terms these days. He must have patience to search for the authentic sources in the authentic idiom. His task is to redeem the alienated Jewish symbol and give it new life. The celluloid Jew is in exile. He has been exploited, sterilized, sentimentalized, vulgarized, but rarely understood. Recent trends in cinema may ultimately free him from the fetters of commercialism. He may benefit from the rising awareness of ethnic individuality in America. A melting pot cinema allowed for very little deviance from the all-American stereotype. Political fears likewise prevented such "deviants" as Sergei Eisenstein, Jules Dassin and lesser known Jewish artists from working in the United States. While Eisenstein has long since died, Dassin has just produced a film on the black ghetto. The latter, himself a veteran of the Yiddish theater, might still realize his dream of filming *The Last of the Just* in his mother tongue. The industry has indeed begun to accommodate itself to the independent artist, the one with enough courage to commit his personal vision to film.

The vision has become distorted. It awaits the conscientious artist who, with uncompromising effort, will fuse prophecy with profanity to create the tension that is art and the ambiguity that is Jewish.

In addition to being a poet, Joel Rosenberg is a graduate of UCLA (Berkeley); he left Hebrew Union College (Reform) to join Havurat Shalom in Boston. In this piece, he has tackled the job of discussing what it means to be a Jewish poet, a task which surely would embarrass and perplex many glib, older critics. While we can find in fiction some works to be called Jewish, the discovery of a Jewish poetic voice has been slow in coming. The essay seems to suggest that what is really necessary to become a Jewish poet is a courageous and risky leap into an encounter with the ambiguities of both language and Jewish experience.

The Jew as Poet:
A Personal Statement[*]

by JOEL ROSENBERG

The poet sooner or later gets around to lamenting that we live in an age when the spoken word no longer counts for much. I have fantasized the bard's time of telling. I have imagined people flocking by the thousands, by the tens of thousands, to hear the poet. I have imagined the opening of his mouth as close to superhuman. I have imagined people hearing and falling to their feet, weeping, vomiting, brought to the threshold of death. I have imagined them rising at the word of the poet to overthrow kings and tyrants. I have imagined them turning on the poet to murder him.

In the Soviet Union, at least, they put their writers in jail. This, to me, is astounding. Not the throwing of people

[*] This selection originally appeared in *Response*, Vol. IV, No. 1, Spring 1970.

into pens and camps, which is never astounding. What is astounding is that a *writer*, of all people, is considered dangerous enough to contain by force. Here in America, we are in a different prison. A writer is sentenced to indifference, to amused or dilettantish curiosity, to analysis by scholars, to interpretation, to admiration. He may write what he wants. He may even cause a soul here and there to tremble. He may even find himself in vogue. But dangerous?

In short, we have a different relationship to words. The temper of our time and place is to words as inflation is to money. Martin Buber has characterized this temper in his explication of Psalm 12. The psalmist, says Buber, is crying out against a "generation of the lie," a time when men have perfected the use of words in the service of lies and trivialities, have accustomed themselves to vain utterances and trivialities, to lips of smoothness, to speaking with "a double heart." Only the pure speech of God can redeem such a setting.[1] It is understandable that, in such a milieu, to follow seriously words spoken in earnest by a poet striving to define his soul, his people, or his time, requires a special effort, perhaps a kind of madness—the sort possessed by people who spend their lives studying English teacups and Hopi *kachina* dolls.

Into this scene steps the Jewish poet. I will not say what is a Jewish poet. This is dangerous, even unethical. Why deny a man even his *pintele* moment with his people? One need not suspend canons of taste. (Who is not weary of endless lyrics "from the Wall," paeans to the *menorah*, laments for the six million, mock-biblical parables, and *Kaddishes* that are not *Kaddishes*?) But one should not, all things heard, define. Let's say that Ginsberg, whose *Kaddish is a Kaddish,* is a Jewish poet, that Leonard Cohen *is* a Jewish poet, though his Jewishness may come forth in his poetry as a finely carved miniature, a conversation piece. By saying simply that a Jewish poet is a Jew who happens to write poetry, we can juxtapose such names as Bialik and Levertov, Tchernikhovsky and Nemerov, Glatstein and Bob Dylan, and savor the irony of the bedfellows we have made. What we *can* define is the very tension, the very polarity (as with all things Jewish) that is carried in the name, "Jewish poet." Two children struggle in Rebekah's womb, "Jewish" and "poet." Can "Jewish," the boundary of boundaries, be one with "poet," the demon who shatters and melts down boundaries? Can "Jewish," the essence of indelible selfhood that neither nation nor Jew has succeeded to erase, coexist with "poet," the restless trier-on of personae? You see, it comes down to that. I suspect you are getting ahead of me at this point. For to be a Jew, *in* the world, *is* to be a poet. For at least a segment of us, poet is a metaphor for Jew, and the reverse.

Thus, I have lamented the passing of the bard. That poetry has lost its communal dimension, has degenerated into private readership (Ginsberg and Yevtushenko at the 92nd Street "Y" notwithstanding) is not to be taken lightly. But even from this role, that of the bard speaking to his people, the poet in us flees, is alienated, is, if I may force the parallel, in *galut* (exile). Arnold J. Band, writing in *Judaism* (Fall, 1965), has wisely pointed out that we have made a stereotype of Jewish poetry as *shira* and *hazon* (song or psalm, and prophetic vision). "It is not easy," Band writes, "to write in competition with Isaiah, Yehudah Ha-Levi, or Bialik." The generation that followed Bialik (and even *that* generation, we see, if we look carefully) shunned the bardlike or prophetic role (say, as well, the role midrashist, and *rebbe*) in favor of an intensely personal, introspective statement. It was precision that counted, not sweep. Here, in fact, was the true test of the Jew's selfhood: if he could write as securely from his vantage point about things human, as his neighbor from his. And when the bard returned, as with Glatstein and other "moderns," it was in the aftermath of you-know-what, and it was humbly, longingly, remorsefully, and *still* introspective:

Nu, bin ich a guter yid?	(Then, am I a good Jew?
Oy vey, tate getrayer,	O, faithful papa,
bin ich a guter yid?	am I a good Jew?
Tchiri bom, tchiri bom,	Tchiri bom, tchiri bom,
bin ich a guter yid?	am I a good Jew?)

Some of us who write poetry go through various phases of poetic identity, sometimes simultaneous. There is the phase of writing about things of "lesser" magnitude: about the alarm clock, about the ear of the man on the subway bench, about the seashell, about getting laid (*as such*). The drive to perfect one's cameos, miniatures, haikus, and graffiti is healthy. It is a part of learning to talk. It may convey a high seriousness. It may succeed in achieving a maximum of meaning with a maximum of economy. Still, there is about this phase an air that is cool and self-centered. We never lose the concern for virtuosity, this first dimension of the poet's development. It dogs us all our days. Included in this dimension is the experimentation with verse forms and inherited styles.

Eventually, one becomes concerned with the challenge of the sustained statement. Occasionally, if we are lucky, things in our vision no longer live as isolated phenomena. Eventually, we reach out over larger areas of time and space, to comprehend the temper of the time. This is the second dimension.

The final dimension is the struggle to transcend ourselves, to create and recapitulate myth and legend, to portray the communal destiny under the aspect of eternity. Here is often concealed the poet's own struggle with the communal will and with the Will that has led him so far afield from casual virtuosity, into realms where words are no longer words, but oracles, *dibbrot*. No poet, Jewish or otherwise, ever fully transcends himself. Writers of greeting-card verse do. Sybils do. Poets don't.

I am intrigued with the possibility of Judaizing the English language. I am intrigued with the possibility that the Orthodox, Hasidic, or other conceivably separatist elements of the Jewish population in America might someday —they should live so long—speak a Judaeo-English or *nayevelt-yiddish,* which may then spill over into mainstream Jewish life. On a literary level, I am interested in the same experimentation in English that Buber and Rosenzweig carried on with German in their translation of the Bible. At present, we are stuck with the problem that any use of a Jewish word, whether Hebrew or Yiddish, smacks of quaintness and self-consciousness. Most of the Jewish words that we can print without italics, like kibbitz, kvetch, and shmaltz, are definitely lowbrow, and, in their present usage, utterly without Jewish significance.

Modern Hebrew poetry is exciting, among other reasons, for the irony and tension it achieves with the use of words that have a simultaneous modern-secular and traditional-sacred connotation, words like *makom* (place; and the Place which contains all places, God), *avodah* (work; and worship), *shaharit* (dawn; and the morning prayer service), or *ein sof* (infinite; or, in Kabbalah, the ultimate, unimaginable identity of God). Thousands of other words evoke associations with Biblical and post-Biblical Jewish history, and with the interplay of Jewish history with the life of alien peoples. How can one even begin to approximate in English the effects achieved by Avot Yeshurun in his poem *"Be-'ir ha-shoftim"* ("In the City of the Judges")? Here, Yeshurun juxtaposes the Hebrew word *tallit* (prayer shawl) with the word *talisma* (talisman, with the echo of the Ashkenazic pronunciation of the word *tallit*) with the words *ta'al isma'* (Arabic for

"Come, hear!"). The words themselves convey the tri-cultural conflict which is the theme of the poem.

This is no mere artifice, even if Yeshurun's application of the pun is a bit strained. Word play is built into the Jewish soul. Hebrew, with its sparse vocabulary and its root family system, allowed one word a host of uses and meanings. Midrash, hermeneutics, and gematria are based on word play. Actually, "play" is somewhat the wrong term. It is "play" only in the sense that free rein is given to the imagination. In truth, it is serious work. The word has legal, and cosmic, importance. The Jewish fascination with words is not just the faculty of sophisticated minds. It permeates proverb, folklore, and popular song. The Hasidim of Menachem Mendel of Kotzk went to their master singing of the holy significance of going to Kotzk on foot (*oyleh regel zan*), as the pilgrim went to Jerusalem on the holy festivals. The song turns on a threefold pun on the word *regel*, which means equally foot, habitual practice, and pilgrim festival. The association of this word (long tied in the Jewish consciousness with the Holy City) with Kotzk has a powerful historical significance. All of this in the mouths of men who were not poets.

But in English? The one non-Semitic word with distinctly Jewish associations, the word "ghetto," has earned its place in the vocabulary of all men, and is no longer a distinctly Jewish word. A few possibilities linger—sweatshop, gas (with some puns in Hebrew), and camp (both concentration and summer). "Temple" may give us some mileage. Synagogue-and-magog may come in handy some day. Beyond this lies a vast vocabulary of respectably Jewish words from Hebrew and Yiddish whose assimilation into English, or Judaeo-English, is presently in a very clumsy grafting stage. A Jewish poetic language in English is in its infancy. I foresee many years of sounding silly.

But on second glance, the possibilities seem endless (if not *eynsofish*), and even a method presents itself. We should be on the lookout in two directions: for words from Jewish tradition and Jewish history that will have interesting and unusual contemporary application; for English renderings of these words and for other English words that have become weighted with strong Jewish associations. Of the first group, there are a host of words that can enter into English the way "shibboleth" entered into seventeenth-century English. See what you can do with: *roeh nolad* (one who sees the event; a perceptive man), *mesiras nefesh* (literally, "handing over one's soul," devotion, commitment), *oyleh regel* (literally, "ascender on foot," pilgrim to Jerusalem; could we use it to mean "peace demonstrator"?). Hint: the application is more striking when it is ironic. Thus, in contemporary Israeli slang, *livdok et ha-shemen,* "to examine the oil," probably a term from the Mishnah, now refers to a form of sexual foreplay. So, we could conceivably call a fool a *mosheh-rabbeynu* ("Moses, our teacher"). A pompous Establishment rabbi could be called a *Shabbat shalom* (these being the only Hebrew words he knows), or a "fur coat" (from a saying of the Kotzker Rebbe's that a generous man warms himself in winter with a fire, which sheds warmth on others; a miserly man, with a fur coat). I shall risk the following:

> Camp is when you test the oil with your girlfriend
> in a sleeping bag in midsummer.
> Old folks remember the war, and before that the good
> times around the radio listening to Roosevelt.
> Camp is
> whom you announce it to with horns.
> Roosevelt was a Jew, if you know what I mean.
> We also made
> lanyards and hung
> whistles on them and wore the lettered T-shirts
> home.
> Going home, we were always tired.
> The lines, the radios. Old songs we remembered.
> Old folks wanting to sleep.
> Camp is sleeping naked with your friends.

What it boils down to is not merely the invention of neologisms, but rather the need to challenge continually the assumptions behind our use of words. In our time our words are *glalim* (smooth stones; turds; *but also:* consequences, that is, potentially full of consequence). We live in ironic times. Our greatest service in ironic times is to revitalize our speech.

Dor, dor, ve-dorshav. Every generation *and* its explicators. But the poet, as Jack Spicer says, "takes too many messages." He is a burned-out radio; a punch-drunk fighter. He crouches at the door of discursiveness. His realm: the unblown bubble, the seed in the moment when it is no longer a seed and not yet a plant, the "nothing," the in-between stage (Maggid of Mezritch). It is wrong to say the poet "writes to solve problems." But he does write to solve what has not yet been formulated as a problem. Flirting with *tohu va-vohu* to wring an ounce of wonder.

I must not, then, spend my seed upon the ground, to formulate prematurely the problems, the themes, the ghosts and angels with which "my generation" (one must pronounce this low and silky) is wrestling in works of the imagination. I have already said too much. There remains a parable and a hint.

The Talmud says that at birth, just before, an angel of silence places a groove above the lips of every man, causing him to grow dumb from the wisdom he has been given, which includes the secrets of the world. Heaven foresees, as well, that the poets are multiplying in the world. The angel of silence is thus well-picked for a poetic whimsicality of his own. For sometimes the angel erases the man's speech. Sometimes the angel erases the man's teachers. Sometimes the angel leaves those intact, but erases the world itself from the man's eyes—removes all things on which the man might look with wonder: all beasts, all dead men, all outcries, all serpents, all beggars, storytellers, and clowns, all tempests, all ash heaps, all saints, cripples, and mutes, all the dried up river beds and consuming fires that would remain in a man's vision after he closes his eyes. The man is left to grow, to live, to eat, to sleep, to love, to be happy, and to die.

Hear, O Brookline, Great Neck, and Beverly Hills! No poet ever fully transcends himself. Writers of greeting-card verse do. Sybils do. Poets don't.

NOTES

1. Yankev Glatstein; *Fun Mayn Gantzer Mi*, New York: 1956, p. 176.

Writing theology is an occupation which seems to have flourished recently, with so many persons finding it easy to affix the title "contemporary theologian" to their curricula vitae. *Theology which arises both out of a personal experience and struggle and out of a devoted immersion in past spiritual history is a rare and happy occurrence. To be personal without being self-indulgent and self-important, on the one hand, and to be authentic without being coldly scientific and scholastic, on the other—such is the challenge. An added danger for Jewish theologians is the temptation to work with the changing categories and trends of young Protestant thinkers, ones which are quite distant from Jewish experience.*

We are fortunate in having in Arthur Green (Itzik Lodzer) not only a theologian who surpasses these standards, but also one who works to realize his vision in the living model of religious community. After graduating from the Jewish Theological Seminary (Conservative), he founded Havurat Shalom Community Seminary (see p. 24, this volume). He is a student of Midrashic, Kabbalistic, and Hasidic sources.

These two essays are profound and imaginative attempts to answer the question of how we experience and deal with holiness. It is significant that the first piece was written in fall, 1967, and the second in the winter of 1970; they reflect, perhaps, a development in religious thinking and experience that is historic and widespread.

Psychedelics and Kabbalah*

by ITZIK LODZER

Mysticism and words are strange bedfellows. They have always had to live together, neither ever being quite comfortable about the presence of the other. Mystics have ever been wary about the limitations of language: words seem to bind them to earth, forcing them to discourse in neatly boxed categories on that which by nature seeks to flow, to soar, transcending all possible verbal boxes. And words, as it were, have always been suspicious of that which they are told they cannot apprehend; they can admit of no reality beyond their own ken.

From the modern mystic's point of view, the most problematic words of all are the words associated with religion. "God," "Holy," "Love"—and all the rest. The words have become prisoners of synagogues and churches where

* This selection originally appeared in *Response,* Vol. II, No. 1, Winter 1968.

their overpowering reality is unknown. So long have they been read responsively that they evoke no response. Even the more sophisticated words now used in their stead suffer from guilt by association; "Numinous" and "Sacred" are too respectable—they turn no one on.

When coming to speak of the deeply religious quality of the experience many of us have had through the use of psychedelic drugs, I balk before conventional religious language. Members of the religious establishment have been too quick to say that any experience brought on by a drug is necessarily cheap. I rather tend to fear the opposite: to speak of psychedelic/mystic experience in terms familiar to religionists might indeed cheapen that experience.

(Now that the mystic in us has voiced his objections and we have duly apologized, we may proceed.)

Perhaps the first key to understanding what psychedelic insight is all about is the notion of *perspective*. Leary, Watts, and others have written at great length about the point of view one achieves during a psychedelic session. In the experience, consciousness and ego become detached. One comes to view the world no longer from the contextual position of the self, but rather as an outsider. "I" can somehow stand aside, somewhere in the back of my head, and watch "me" at play. The "I" who watches is liberated from the context of the "me" who acts. Associated with this generally cute busybody "me" (who sometimes seems to belong to the kind of toy world one sees when taking off in an airplane) is the entire active material universe: on the side of the "I," to one of a Western background, stands He who looks on from beyond. The most distinctively non-Western aspect of this God-image, incidentally, is that here He who looks from beyond cannot suppress a smile. The world is simply much too cute to be an object of cosmic wrath. Visions of the laughing Buddha who knows it's all a joke . . .

Together we look from beyond. God and I are not yet

one at this point, but I have taken the first step: I am learning to see things from his point of view. That which I thought was all terribly real just a few moments ago now seems to be part of a great dramatic role-playing situation, a cosmic comedy which this "me" has to play out for the benefit of his audience. I am overwhelmed by my dramatic style, and the world's. I suppress my desire to applaud, waiting patiently for the end of the act. I no longer think that anything is "real" down there on stage, but I feel truly awed by the artistry of it all.

This perspective has a particularly close analogue in the history of Jewish thought. One of the great systems of *HaBaD* mysticisms is that of Reb Aaron of Starroselje, who bases much of his thought on a distinction between truths and realities "from God's point of view" and "from man's point of view." Reb Aaron hesitates, along with so many other Western mystics, to call our world of time and space mere illusion. (The Zohar, in calling the universe of ordinary consciousness the *Alma-De-Shikra* or World of Deception, is more radical here.) Rather, says Reb Aaron, we must learn to speak of two levels of reality. In order for "down" consciousness to function, this world must be seen as somehow real. From man's point of view, time, space, selfhood, and God's otherness are all to be taken quite seriously. Seen from beyond, however, world and ego are but aspects of the same illusion. From God's point of view, only God can be called real. The mystic must learn to balance himself between the two standpoints, never falling *too* far off the tightrope into either one. Of course the Kabbalist would never have been so immodest as to tell us openly that he personally had been "high" enough to see the world from God's point of view. He doesn't have to tell us. Assuming that the Jewish mystical literature embodies real inner experience and not just a body of empty theosophic doctrine (and this is my assumption throughout), the point is quite obvious: with the proper pneumatic

keys, man can come to see the world as it is viewed from
above. One who has read Alan Watts' description of psychedelic experience in *The Joyous Cosmology* might feel
much at home with Reb Aaron.

Now the serious Jewish theologian might rise in protest: How can you dare to equate the vision of Reb Aaron,
who labored humbly for years and meant his system to
encompass answers to timeless theological issues, with
something you describe in such terribly frivolous terms? I
would admit, of course, that there is a tremendous difference *in tone* between the writings of the Kabbalist and
that which we seem to experience. This is precisely one of
the great advantages or drawbacks of psychedelics, depending upon where you stand. Because mystic insight
came so hard to most mystics, their words came out heavy
and awesomely serious. Only a rare figure, a Bratzlaver for
example, could make his theology dance. But when one
can flip into mystic consciousness as easily as one swallows
a pill, the whole thing is so much lighter that it almost cannot be "serious." Indeed, nothing *remains* serious: on the
next wave of acid one can flip out again, go another rung
higher, and watch Reb Aaron's system too become part of
the Joke.

Turning now from a description of psychedelic perspective to a discussion of the *content* of the religious insight
that comes to the psychedelic voyager, our first encounter
is with the age-old metaphysical/mystical problem of the
nature of change. As we step back and view the world
as outsiders, we observe that everything about us, including our own selves, is involved in a seemingly never-
ending flow. All is becoming, moving. I blink my eyes
and seem to reopen them to an entirely new universe,
one terribly different from that which existed a moment
ago. I think of Hesse's image of the river of life with its

countless changing forms. Yes, but at the same time one seeks a metaphor that makes for bolder colors. Everything that is stands constantly ready to reorganize itself into new molecular patterns, to burst into hitherto undreamed-of forms of life. Kaplan's "God as Process" becomes attractive (has he been there?), but only for a moment. For behind the constantly changing patterns of reality, or—better—within them, something remains the same. If there is a "God" we have discovered through psychedelics, He is the One within the many; the changeless constant in a world of change.

On one level I perceive this duality through the perception of external (or relatively external!) phenomena: the face of the friend in front of me may change a million times, may become all faces or may become The Face. All this *happens*—I do not *experience* it as "hallucination"—yet somewhere in the bottom of my consciousness I know that before me stands my friend, unchanged. *Everything has been changing, but nothing has changed*. On a still more profound level, one experiences this paradox of change and constancy with regard to oneself. I encounter my own consciousness at any given moment in a psychedelic voyage only in terms of its contents. My mind, now more than at any other time, is filled to overflowing with fast changing images and countless interweaving patterns. In the face of this, the continuity of consciousness from one moment to the next is to me the greatest of miracles. All is changing, and my mind seems constantly on the verge of bursting into the shrapnel of its own perceptions —and yet somehow "I" remain. Space, time, and consciousness, insofar as they can be distinguished from one another, are all going through this same infinitely majestic but terrifying process; they are all rushing constantly toward the brink of "Bang!" disintegration, but just as they reach the far limits of existence they turn around and smile. Relax; we haven't moved at all *Olam—Shanah—*

Nefesh; Space, Time, and Mind, says the *Sefer Yetsirah,* are playing the same games. The miracle of how all three remain constant in their change, how their oneness persists through their never ending multiplicity of forms, is the essence of religious wonder. Somehow the Principle of Paradox which allows for this coexistence seems to want to be capitalized. . . .

Now it seems to this reader of the Jewish mystical literature that here we have encountered one of the basic motifs of Kabbalistic thought. The Kabbalah speaks of two aspects of the divine Self: *Eyn Sof* or "The Endless," and the *Sefirot,* the various aspects of God's active inner life. Insofar as God is seen as *Eyn Sof,* he is in no way subject to change or multiplicity. He is eternal oneness, possessing no attributes, no personality, no specific content of any kind. And, in a certain sense, He is all there is. The seeming reality of God as *Sefirot,* let alone the illusory reality of this "World of Deception," are nothing in the face of the One. It is only through the veiledness of the One that the many are granted some form of existence. The enlightened are at moments able to peer through the veils and catch a glimpse of the Reality within. Insofar as God is the *Sefirot,* on the other hand, the near antithesis is true. In the Kabbalists' descriptions of God as *Sefirot* we find a brightly colored picture of infinitely varied forms of divine life. God loves, gives birth, is Himself born, unites and separates, pours forth multicolored light and withholds it when it becomes too strong, tragically causes and then combats evil, etc., etc. While *nothing* can be said of God as *Eyn Sof,* virtually *everything* can be said of God as *Sefirot.* Here there is no limit to the ever-flowing and ever-changing face of the divine personality. God as *Sefirot* is in a sense closer to the dancing multi-limbed gods of the Hindu myths than He is to the heavy seated God of the West, who only by cosmic Herculean effort can be moved from the Throne of Justice to the Throne of Mercy. Countless images can be used to describe the *Sefirot* aspect of the Divine. God is water: the various aspects of His self are streams and rivers flowing into the cosmic sea. God is fire: the blue and the red of the candle's flame unite and rise into unlimited divine white. God is speech: from the hidden chasms of heart and throat, the Word struggles forth to emerge from the lips. Perhaps most striking: God is male and female, eternally seeking self-fulfillment through a union that has been rent asunder. In short, the Kabbalistic description of the two faces of God seems strikingly similar to that which we have met in the psychedelic experience. Reality is many-faced and ever-changing, and yet the One behind it all remains the same.

Students of the Kabbalah have generally shied away from this kind of experiential analysis of the Kabbalistic God-image. Those trained in *Religionsgeschichte* have seen the duality of *Eyn Sof* and *Sefirot* as a historic combining of Neoplatonic and Gnostic conceptions. Others, proceeding from a more philosophical background, have viewed this duality as an attempt to solve the *philosophic* problem of how the many proceed from the One. But since we are after all dealing with *mystics,* an explanation which takes the inner experience of the mystic into account might prove to be more fruitful. Our claim here, of course, is that on this level one can learn of the classic mystical experience from the psychedelic. When we further compare both the psychedelic reports and the Kabbalistic doctrine with the myths of oneness and change in Hindu mysticism, we can only conclude that psychedelic experiments have indeed led us to one of the major mystic insights common to East and West.

Within the context of this same distinction between *Eyn Sof* and *Sefirot* in God, we might mention another parallel we find between Kabbalistic Judaism and the religious viewpoint that seems to be emerging from psychedelic experimentation. As we have seen, the Kabbalists were hardly afraid of using imagery in speaking of God. On the contrary, they were far more daring and creative in their use of religious imagery than Judaism had ever been. Yet they knew enough to maintain a free-flowing attitude toward their own metaphoric creations. Images in Kabbalistic literature are beautifully inconsistent. Intentionally mixed metaphors abound in the Zohar: in the midst of a passage describing the *Sefirot* as patterns of light, the light imagery will suddenly turn sexual; at other times, human imagery will quietly dissolve into images of water. They tacitly knew well that all their images were of value—and that none of them was itself the truth. The anonymous mystic who penned the *Shir-Ha-Kavod* knew this well:

> They imaged You, but not as You are;
> They adjudged You only through Your deeds.
> They conceived of You through many visions,
> Yet You remain One, within all the images.

Images of the *Sefirot* could be taken seriously without being meant literally; for *Eyn Sof* itself, no images were allowed at all. As a matter of fact, the taking of any image for God too literally, or the divorcing of a particular image from its intentionally amorphous context, was considered by the Kabbalist to be the very heart of idolatry. The Kabbalist's consciousness was sufficiently expanded (an expression often found in the later Kabbalistic literature: *Gadlut Ha-Mohin*) that he could see through his own image games.

Similar processes seem to be a common part of the psychedelic voyage. At various stages of increasingly intensified consciousness almost anything that catches the traveler's eye can be converted into a metaphor which for the moment seems tremendously rich and significant. Looking at a picture, contemplating a certain word—suddenly we understand what it is "all" about. Like the author of the Zohar looking into the candle and suddenly discovering a new way of expressing the Great Truth, the psychedelic voyager, if he allows himself to "groove" on almost anything for a while, may come up with an image which produces great excitement. Indeed, this is one of the great "pastimes" of people under the influence of psychedelics: the construction of elaborate and often beautiful systems of imagery which momentarily seem to contain all the meaning of life or the secrets of all the universe, only to push beyond them moments later, leaving their remains as desolate as the ruins of a child's castle in the sand. No metaphor is permanent; one can always ascend another rung and look down on the silliness of what appeared to be revelation just minutes before. Most important, in this potentially constant drive upward, out-shooting all images, one can catch a glimpse of what the Kabbalists must have *experienced* as *Eyn Sof*: expanded consciousness seems to have no limit, except that of the degree of intensity that the mind can stand. Reb Nachman Bratzlaver speaks of this in startlingly contemporary language: the mind is expanded to the point where it becomes limitless (*Eyn Sof* is the term he uses!), and it has difficulty *fitting* into the brain when it seeks to return. Now again we have a difference in the degree of serious-ness with which the whole mystic venture is taken. For the classic Kabbalist the images of his tradition were, if not absolute truth, nevertheless eternally valid approxima-tions of aspects of the divine reality. For contemporary trippers, for whom all this happens so much more quickly, similar images may be nothing more than a moment's heavenly entertainment. But this in no way contradicts the impression that the states of consciousness reached are in some manner the same. Both find that image and meta-phor are the only tools that language can offer them which may be of value, yet as both confront the Ultimate they are forced to leave all images behind.

It is in part for this very reason, so well comprehended

by Western mystics, that most psychedelic voyagers have sought their religious guidance in the traditions of the East. In the East, the distinction between image and reality appears to have been better preserved, at least in such "intellectual" circles as those around Vedanta and Zen. Both Judaism and Christianity, as taught and practiced in the last few centuries, have neglected some of the most sophisticated elements of their own traditions, including some of those insights which would be of greatest value to us today. Judaism as presented today knows nothing of God as *Eyn Sof;* it has lost the creative mystic drive which led beyond its own images into a confrontation with the Nothing. The Judaism which contemporary Jews have inherited is one of a father figure who looms so large that one dare not *try* to look beyond Him. We have indeed become trapped by our image. The Kabbalists knew well that God-as-father made sense only in the context of God-as-mother, God-as-lover, God-as-bride, etc. They played the image game with great delicacy; their descendants have forgotten how to play. Perhaps most tragically of all, the Father Himself has lost His power. Were it not for guilt feelings and some sentimentalism on the part of His most loyal children, He might have been put to pasture long ago. Sophisticated Eastern religionists never took their god-images so seriously that they had to undergo the trauma of their decay and death.

From the perspective of this psychedelic/mystic insight, conventional Western religion seems to have fallen prey to a psychologically highly complex idolatry. In Judaism, the cult of God-as-father has been allowed to run rampant for hundreds of years. Now that the image is crumbling, Western man naively seems to think that the religious reality is itself about to die. Indeed, he has forgotten that there ever was a reality behind his image.

Deeply tied to this problem of image, father image, and
religious reality is the whole question of inner freedom
in the religious consciousness. The psychedelic experience is generally conceived of as terribly exhilarating
liberation. When one allows oneself to ascend into the
rungs of consciousness associated with "God's point of
view," one releases oneself from the bondage of all those
daily ego problems which until now had seemed so terribly important. Conventional strivings for achievement or
success seem to have been just so many meaningless webs
in which the Self had become entangled. Now one can see
beyond them, and their emptiness lies bared. This is of
course the real meaning of "dropping out" in Leary's slo-
gan. In the face of the magnificent reality now revealed to
me, I am truly amazed that just yesterday my ego was
frantic about the silliest things imaginable. I try to recon-
struct my life on the basis of this psychedelically induced
moment of truth. I resolve to stay out of bags, to maintain
this freedom from the trivial as I re-enter my former
worlds.

Mystics of all traditions have experienced this same
liberation. In Judaism it is a part of the "negation of the
Is" (*Bitul he-Yesh*), or it is sometimes more specifically
referred to as the "stripping off of the physical" (*Hitpash-
tut ha-Gashmiyut*). The voyager reaches the rungs where
all his physical needs, all his this-worldly preoccupations,
are left behind. They no longer matter to him; their vanity
has been revealed. This, for example, is the interpretation
that some of the Kabbalists give to the act of fasting on
Yom Kippur: on the day of the great confrontation, man
transcends his own physical self. He has become angelic;
that is to say, he has been liberated from his ordinary
earthbound context. This of course is virtually the antithesis of the way *Yom Kippur* is seen in non-mystical Jewish

theology. Yet generally for the Jewish mystic this liberation is carefully held in check. In the Jew's relationship
to God, the image of *serving* was of tremendous power.
Man's mystic liberation was not allowed to flourish for its
own sake. Rather it was to permit him, by throwing off the
yoke of enslavement to this world, to take upon himself
the yoke of service of the kingdom of heaven. This is not
to say, of course, that there is no joy in real Jewish worship. Jews knew well how to "serve the Lord with glad-
ness." But for the modern man seeking mystic awareness
of the Divine, the image of master and servant is as dead
as that of father and child. The nature of our religious encounter, even if it is mystic, cannot counter the fact that
we are children of the post-Nietzschean world: we want
to enjoy and exult in our liberation no less than others
who proclaim the "death of God." Our particular form of
the awareness of God can no longer be one that leads us
to His *service*.

This is not to say that none of the traditional forms of
Jewish religious expression can be made to work. In the
spirit of Berdyczewski, Kaplan, and Richard Rubenstein, I
too believe that certain symbols can be reborn if we allow
them to undergo a *basic reorientation* in meaning. The attempt to instill the liberating effects of psychedelic consciousness into everyday life generally meets with, at best,
limited success. One has the feeling that the absence of
ritual makes this effort all the more difficult. Were the
great ritual moments of Judaism used as reminders (or re-
creators) of states of elevated consciousness, as they once
were used to some extent by the Kabbalists, those of us
who have gained religious insight through the use of drugs
might indeed find great excitement in the ritual life. Com-
pulsive or legalistic attitudes toward ritual we will of
course find repulsive; ritual must help us to be more free,
not bind us. Those of us who do know of the gentle poetry
that is still to be found in the Sabbath and the Holy Days

would like to open up to that poetry, seeking in it the reflection of what we have discovered within. We are wary of being "hooked," or of being tied into a religious community with which we have terribly little in common—but we do want to try.

Of particular relevance here are those rituals which have so much to do with the sacred in time. The religious view of sacred time, so essential to Judaism and yet so alien to the modern—even observant—Jew, finds its parallel deeply engrained in the psychedelic experience. As with the Hasidic Sabbath, time in psychedelic consciousness takes on a cosmic co-ordinate. The moment exists, but eternity is mysteriously contained within it. A psychedelic voyager, watching a sunrise in the woods, told me that he *knew* how Adam felt when the sun first rose in Eden. Eden was there with him; he was back at home in Eden. Watching a waterfall in New Jersey, hearing it crash through the silence, we were reminded of a midrash that speaks of the silence that surrounded revelation, and suddenly we stood at the foot of the eternal Sinai. An almost sexual (in its shocking flow of completeness) union of moment and eternity, of the here and now with the everywhere and forever, is constantly taking place. But of course. This is again one of the things that Kabbalistic theology is all about. Creation happened; creation *was a moment*. Yet creation still happens. All future moments were contained within creation, and creation is renewed in every moment since. God "renews every day the work of creation." In the Kabbalistic view, Being flows unceasingly from the Endless, through the chasm of the Nothing, into ever-new forms of life. The world in which the Kabbalist lives is, in one of his greatest symbols, a universe of eternal birth.

This is perhaps even more true of Sinai. On a certain day in the third month after the Children of Israel had left Egypt, God who is "beyond time" and who is Himself called "Place" for He is beyond the totality of place, came down upon the mountain. Cosmic space and endless time enter into union with the here and now. And then, because of that union, Sinai becomes a moment that can live forever. Every moment and every place, according to Hasidic doctrine, contains within itself a Sinai waiting to be discovered. The Torah is ever being given; the moment of Sinai, having tasted of eternity, can never die. One feels that certain of the Hasidic masters would have smilingly understood: watching the silence and rush of a waterfall in New Jersey, we stood before Sinai.

The eternal moment. Having been given ringside seats from which to witness the struggle, dance, and ultimate union of the Forever and the Now, we have the exhilarating feeling of having seen through a great illusion. We had been taking time so *seriously* until now; suddenly, having peered through to eternity, time has become a joke.

We live in temporal and trans-temporal realities at once. All that we have said with regard to constancy and change seems to apply equally to eternity and time. Both are fulfilled through their union. Alan Watts describes the experience this way: "At some time in the middle of the twentieth century, upon an afternoon in the summer, we are sitting around a table on the terrace, eating dark homemade bread and drinking white wine. And yet we seem to have been there forever, for the people with me are no longer the humdrum and harassed little personalities with names, addresses, and social security numbers—the specifically dated mortals we are all pretending to be. They rather appear as immortal archetypes of themselves without, however, losing their humanity. . . . They are at once unique and eternal, men and women but also gods and goddesses. For now that we have time to look at each other, we have become timeless."

"We have become timeless. . . ." Israel, through celebrating the Sabbath and fulfilling the Torah, achieves a state which is "beyond time," as is God Himself. An old Hasidic doctrine is strangely rediscovered and relived by Watts. Were those aspects of Jewish life that were once purported to be relevant to states of higher consciousness only *translated* into a symbolic language our age could read, the Jewish scene might begin to look significantly different.

As we turn to a discussion of the deepest, simplest, and most radical insight of psychedelic/mystic consciousness, we balk before the enormous difficulty of expressing it in terms that will not be offensive to the Western man, and particularly to the religiously sensitive Jew. This insight has been so terribly frightening to the Jewish consciousness, so bizarre in terms of the Biblical background of all Jewish faith, that even the mystics who knew it well generally fled from fully spelling it out. We refer of course to the realization that all reality is one with the Divine. *Tat tvam asi,* in Hinduism: "Thou are God." The Hindu mystic says it unabashedly: Self and self flow together; Atman and Brahman are one. The game of Western consciousness, including most of Western religion, is truly threatened by such a claim. We have built all of our colossal civilization on the premise of the reality of the individual ego; our very religion and ethics assign limitless importance to the decisions and confrontations of the separate human self. Judaism from the Bible down to Buber and Rosenzweig has been the religion of God's *dialogue* and *confrontation* with man. If God and man are truly one—if separate identity is really but a veiling of our true oneness—what has all the game been for?

The question is more urgent than just one of institutional vested interest. Our very notion of sanity in the Western world is here being called into question. If the self and its everyday vision are said to be illusion (or at best half-truth), what place is left for sanity as the ability to distinguish the "fantastic" from the "real"? If inner vision (drug-induced or not) is to replace sense perception as the most appropriate vehicle for man's apprehension of "reality," is not the psychotic perhaps the most enlightened of us all? These questions have deeply bothered both classic and modern mystics—as well as their detractors. They certainly form the basis for the classic Jewish fears of mystic study affecting or "burning" the unstable and the young; they also legitimately enter into the reasoning of those who demand sensible societal controls of the use of psychedelic drugs.

And yet, despite all the fears and reservations, the feeling of the true oneness of God and man is encountered with surprising frequency in the literature of the Kabbalah. The *Shechinah,* the last of the ten *Sefirot* within God, also contains all the lower worlds within itself. As God achieves His own inner unity, all the worlds, experimentally implying the mystic's own soul as well, enter into the cosmic One. The human soul, according to mystic doctrine, is in some particular way "a part of God above." In an oft-repeated parable of early Hasidic literature, the true son of the King, when entering his Father's palace, discovers that the very palace itself, insofar as its chambers separated him from his father, is mere illusion. Scholem describes the stage in Zohar's thinking at which the human "I" becomes but an echo of the divine "I": "the point where man, in attaining the deepest understanding of his own self, becomes aware of the presence of God."

In a particularly poignant passage, and a most revealing one in terms of classic Jewish hesitation before the identity of God and self, the Maggid of Mezritch asks God, as it were, to step outside of man for a moment, so that man can play the confrontation game. To paraphrase him: "I know that I have no real existence outside You, but there are times when my needs require that I feel I am standing before You. Let me be for a few months, so that I can ask You to judge me, without Your having to judge Yourself."

Psychedelic consciousness knows this experience. We too, like our mystic forebearers, are overwhelmed, exhilarated, and frightened by the knowledge. There are times when we want to shout it in the streets, to turn men on to the awareness that all of them are God. There are also times when we want to come back, to live in the world where man is man. In order to do this, we are even willing to pretend that man is man and God is God. But we know that this is a game; we cannot retract. Because we have the *hubris* to admit to ourselves that we have been there, we are doomed to live here with a boundless liberating joy that we fear to express, lest we be seen as madmen.

But even then we have a role to play. Our society suffers greatly from a lack of madmen.

Nikos Kazantzakis speaks of man's search for God as an ascent up a seemingly unassailable mountain. Men have been climbing for countless generations; occasionally one of them comes to face the summit. There are ledges and cliffs. The higher one goes, the greater the danger of falling. Our forefathers were experts at climbing the mountain. Kabbalists generally climbed slowly, deliberately, step after sure-footed step. They were equipped with road maps that had been tested and found good for centuries. Nearly every inch of the mountain was charted. If there occasionally was a slip-up, it was usually by one of those who tried to chart a bit of a new path for himself. The task was formidable: many tried, some fell, but a good number came near to their particular summits.

Today we no longer know how to read the road maps. In any case, they would do us little good. They were charted for hikers. We are driving up the mountain in a fast car, equipped with brightly flashing multicolored headlights. We will get there faster and more easily—if we get there at all.

Perhaps you will pray for us back in our village in the valley. Strange: up there, high on the slopes of the mountain, we seem to forget how to pray. . . .

After Itzik: Toward a Theology of Jewish Spirituality

by ARTHUR GREEN

[*for H.L. & S.Z.*]

Introduction I

Denizens of two worlds have never been happy creatures. Climbing half out of their own skins in an attempt to wholly enter one world or the other has always seemed to them artificial; the attempt at a personal wholeness based on an acceptance, on the other hand, of their dual status, or even a glorification of it, often strikes them as insufficiently real. So it is with the demons of Isaac Bashevis Singer: human in the nether world and demonic in the human world, at home in neither and nowhere at rest.

Such a creature, insofar as he seeks out the life of the spirit, is man. "Half from the upper realms, half from the lower . . ." not quite at home, we might add, in heaven or earth. The spiritual history of man can be read as nothing but a series of attempts at resolution of the internalized conflicts between worlds and life-styles above and below. Reconciliation of heaven and earth: the point where mystical union *is* personal integration. Yet instead, we try to opt for one or the other. Alas. Man's attempts both to become angel and to deny the angelic in himself may have occasioned great bales of cosmic laughter and an infinite flow of heavenly tears, but they have left us no less fragmented than before.

Once there was a moment of conversion, of knowing, of *da'at* in that most intimate sense that "above" and "below" were silly attempts at distinction, that God flows into man and man into God so fully that to try to pull them apart could only do violence to both. No, not a "moment of conversion"—many such moments, perhaps, and none of them quite conversionary. That indeed is our problem and the question with which we begin: Is conversion any longer possible for those who have so nearly been converted so often, and in whom there thus remains so little innocence?

Introduction II

"Open for me the gates of righteousness . . ." says the psalmist. "I come through them and praise the Lord." Standing at the gate, looking through to the other side. Peering into Wonderland. Waiting. Joseph K. before the Law. Open them *for* me.

Open them for yourself, damn you! Push! "What are you hollering at Me for?" God says to Moses. You think *I* open the gates for anyone? "Tell the children of Israel to get moving!"

> ". . . and sometimes it happens that a
> man's turning begins not on his own
> account. Rather he is awakened to
> the turning by an awesome Presence
> which God in His bounty brings to him . . .
> Now this Awe comes from Above, and
> therefore it cannot last forever. If
> it were indeed to last, that man's ser-
> vice would be only of that which comes

from God Himself. Thus he takes away
that Awe which he had granted him, so
that man will go build up his own love
of God. Then his service will truly
be of his own . . . This doesn't come to
man easily; it's a matter of great
strength and concentration over long
periods of time. When a man seeks
love in this way and doesn't find it,
he may cry out to God to help him as
he had before. Such a prayer is not
answered. A man just has to work on
it on his own . . ."

Thus far a voice from the eighteenth century.[1] That
which you don't work out on your own, in a struggle that
has to begin way down here in the world of ordinary
weekday consciousness, somehow just isn't going to last.
That doesn't mean the first moment (drug-induced or not)
was any less real, but it does let you know that it can't
become the replacement for down here religious struggle.

Struggle. Storm the gates. No, you don't have to: a
gentle push will do. Now why don't we open them ourselves? If the gates are there before us, and we're standing
so close we can even see how they open—and we've even
looked through them—

> Try to run . . . try to hide
> Break on through to the other side!

We stand dumbstruck both before the gates and before
the question. We remain afraid. At Sinai we said to Moses:
"You go talk to that thing, man. You tell us what it says.
We're not gettin' any closer . . ."

When I ask myself these days who we, Israel, are, I hear
myself answering: "We are those who fled from Sinai."

Now that is really a bit of shorthand, a one part reduction of a two part statement: "We are those who were there at Sinai and who fled." (One who has not been there of course has no need to flee. He may be involved in some other flight and flatter himself by thinking that it is Sinai he flees, but his confusion can be seen and his error felt. Still, the myth of the faith-community retains its meaning: On some other plane *all* of us Israelites have been to Sinai and fled.) I would want to reintegrate the flight from Sinai into our spiritual history, from which it has been largely expunged. We generally choose to see ourselves as those to whom God spoke, as those who listened, those who agreed (perhaps the word is "acquiesced"). But that should not be all . . . we are also those who fled. This does not make us the accursed of God in any very particularistic sense; it simply makes us human. Restating firmly that at Sinai we were mere terrified mortals might give us a more complete and realistic spiritual self-image, one of less angelic perfection but one with which we might more readily identify: "We are those who stood at Sinai, who saw and heard, were scared out of our little minds (*mohin de qatnut*), and fled!"

This, you see, is why we are eternally Israel, those who wrestle with the Divine. Our faith is not one that hopes to reside in bliss, but rather one committed to movement and struggle. Committed and destined; I'd want to say both. Committed to struggle, because the ascent to the Endless is itself Endless[2] and we are constantly to see ourselves as climbing up Jacob's ladder, not satisfied to stand on *any* rung.[3] And destined to struggle? Because we're always falling off and starting the ascent all over again. Falling off the ladder because we refuse to ascend (each rung is only strong enough to hold you for an instant) and because of our constant silly habit of looking down and contemplating flight.

We are Israel in that life in the Presence will always be

a struggle for us. The discovery of God comes to us as a
constant surprise, almost a shock. For countless generations we chant: "the whole earth is full of his glory," yet
each time we turn around and see the glory of God in a
new place we shudder with a mixture of delight, fear, and
astonishment. Our sense of wonder is always getting lost.
The shallow rationalist bias creeps back in, sits tight and
waits to be blasted sky-high again before he'll budge an
inch. Something in us is constantly repeating the primal
conflict of the Israelite Moses: "C'mon, stop wasting your
time" the over-educated Jewish boy in him must have
been saying. "A plain ordinary thornbush and a little desert
heat. Optical illusion." But Moses is, after all, Moses, and
there has to be a story. He turned aside to look. He
stopped, and there was God. He looked for a minute, saw
and heard, and then, like one who still half thought he
wouldn't be able to stand it (or perhaps feared that he
would be able to stand it?), he hid his face.

"You want to know what a *zaddik* is?" asks Reb
Hayyim Haikl of Amdur. "We ordinary men need the
hiding, we need to have God hide His light from us. The
zaddik says "No!" to hiding and stares right into the
sun!" [4] Moses, *even Moses,* hid his face and said: "How
about sending someone else?"

Brinksmanship, unspeakable risk, borderline madness
of intensity and blindness of immersion—those are the
things it takes to be a *zaddik.* Most of us Jews prefer to be
beynonim, plain humans, ever living in the stream of our
particular dialectical movement, confronting and hiding,
moments of Presence followed in rapid succession by moments of dryness and despair. In other generations the
cyclical motion was interpreted differently, but our particular version of it seems to run something like this: disbelief, seduction, wonder, living-in-the-Presence, terror,
flight, disbelief, and so on and so forth. Each moment in
the cycle is tyrannical and dogmatic: disbelief has no faith

in the rebirth of wonder, and in our moments of living in the Presence we are revolted by the cynicism and self-conscious secularism of our unbelieving periods. The twentieth-century *beynoni* lives as though bound to the cycle of wonder and doubt.

We do not seek liberation by means of breaking out of the cycle. Opting for either world, as we have said, can only lead to prolonging of fragmentation. We see spiritual ebb and flow, moments of absence and moments of Presence, as central to the human religious situation. Our desire is neither to deny nor to escape it, but rather to learn to live as religious human beings in our moments of spiritual ebb. What else can be done with the moment of disbelief in our cycle? If we are not to deny the cycle altogether, must we allow ourselves to ever be torn apart by shallow cynicisms that we should like to have transcended long ago? Can there be spiritual growth if there has to be constant return to such a coarse moment of ebb? Most basically: in viewing the ebb and flow of the Spirit's presence within us, can we step beyond conflict and see the thing as rhythm, as a rhythmic movement that brings some *excitement* to the spiritual life and inspiration to the "downs" as well as the "ups"?

Hasidic theological texts, which comprise the literature we have that is most attuned to the problems of spiritual quest, knew this problem well. *Razo wa-shov,* they called it. "Running back and forth." Man runs back and forth, in and out of the divine Presence, and the Presence itself (*hiyyuth*) seems to be running back and forth, in and out of the human soul. In Hasidic terms, it seems to be largely the movement of the Spirit itself that creates the spiritual cycle. Ultimate conversion is not to be made easy for us. At the same time, the spiritual masters of the Hasidic tradition, perhaps partly through the very term *razo wa-shov,* which allowed them a theologization of the spiritual reality, were able to live with the cyclical movement and continue to build. This, then, is what we seek to articulate: a contemporary theology of *razo wa-shov*.

There was a time when the appropriate geographical metaphor for our spiritual lives seemed to be one of isolated, widely separated peaks set in the midst of broad extended flatlands. The task we then set for ourselves was that of ascending the mountain with some measure of safety to bring down its secret, hoping thereby to give some light to the vast and empty world of the everyday. Then we were rather sure that we wanted to begin with the highs, that they were the paradigm of religious awareness after which the everyday was to be remodeled. If one will permit a rather simplistic reading of the tradition, a kind of *Shabbat* and weekday model, where one clearly knows which are the peaks and which are the valleys. The goal: "the world that is wholly *Shabbos*." But the humdrum world persists; the weekday simply doesn't want to become *Shabbos*! To make *Shabbos* the model for a respiritualized weekday is eschatological. In our schema it would mean a breaking out of the cycle, a radical spiritualism that would deny legitimacy to moments of *qatnut*, of spiritual ebb.

We do not always live in the glow of spiritual *Shabbos*. When we don't, we have to begin from below.[5] There is no upper light flowing into us; we have only the world. The discovery of the Presence in the world below, in the very earthiness of the weekday, then becomes our task. This is the time of struggle, the time of *avodah* as active work in seeking out one's religious way *in the world*. We do not mean by this an indiscriminating embrace of the secular, which has come to characterize the religious stance of a good many contemporary Christians. They (like the kibbutzniks, as Rav Kuk would say) have good reason to be in rebellion against an anti-worldly spiritualism. We mean rather a more profound fusion of the religious and the secular, one which can turn inward to a real spiritual life partly in order to nurture the outer life and one which labors with love in the secular world without granting it *ultimate* seriousness.

Religious work in the weekday world, as we would see it today, must proceed from that element within the Hasidic tradition which sought to deny the separability of matter and spirit.[6] We are not interested in redeeming the spark from any earthly prison; we need rather to discover that all is spark. Nor do we seek to rejoice in the transparency or "illusion" of material reality.[7] We do not experience ourselves or one another as body and soul, but as bodysoul; so too with matter and spirit. We seek our exultation in the spirit that can be known in the very flesh of the material world. "The breath of all life . . . and the spirit of all flesh."

This is the quality of *razo wa-shov* that we are after, that which is most faithful both to our own perceptions and to the ongoing specific mission of Israel in the history of Western spirituality. We are Israel in that we know and insist upon the oneness of matter and spirit.[8] Sometimes we are convinced of the utter folly of such a position with its inherent optimism, yet we will not let go. Sometimes all of Jewish history seems to us one vast plot by which the nations of the world hope to convert us to their otherworldliness, making it more than painfully obvious that salvation is not to be found in this life, that the true realm of the spirit must be elsewhere. No avail; we dig in and hold on to earth. Our *razo wa-shov* is not to be seen only as a ladder; in moments of stress the picture is turned on its side and the Jew is seen scurrying back and forth across a tightrope stretched out between matter and spirit, desperately patching things up at one end or the other. Even when the link appears to be so terribly tenuous, we dare not pronounce it broken.

The transformation of the ebb into a moment of religious legitimacy may take countless forms. The *via activa* as one side of the spiritual life, recognizing itself as not more and no less than that, may then rightly seek its fulfillment through social concern and political involvement. The kinds of political stances that would emerge as expressions of the spiritual as we see it can of course not be specifically pre-determined, but would have a good deal to do both with the maximizing of human freedom and the pursuit of peace. For others the active life could involve teaching, involvement in the personal and religious growth of others: the special concern we develop for student-comrades. Still others might find their fulfillment in the redemptive robustness of physical labor, particularly such as would involve them with the realms of animal and plant.

Through all of this, the maintaining of religious perspective will be essential, and will be an uphill struggle. If the Presence is to be rediscovered in the weekday world, demands will be made upon us that will radically re-orient the direction of our lives—demands of discipline of lifestyle, of ritual patterns and interpersonal openness which hardly thrive in the context of the mechanized, isolated, and frightened lives of the American middle class. The work of redemption, no matter what form it takes, will require new and intimate communities of support, which live outside current standards of achievement and success. We would do well to look at the vows of poverty found in monastic life, though seeking to read them somewhat more broadly than has been done in the past.

Such a religious path, if not watered down to absurdity, will speak only to very few. That is for the good. Ours is not an age in which popular spiritual movements could escape terrible perversion. Just as there are moments of ebb and flow in the individual's spiritual life, there at times appear to be historical periods of ebb and flow in mankind's general awareness of the Spirit. If we are to survive this great age of spiritual ebb, it will only be by the creation of small but terribly significant religious elites who can plant the seed for what may be some more fruitful future generation.

Even for the few, the task remains formidable. Our membership cards in the Western intellectual community are parted with only with the greatest difficulty. We cannot proclaim ourselves to be traditional believers; it is hoped that we are too honest even to try to talk ourselves into that position. The fragmentation of truth is part of our legacy as twentieth-century men. Yet maintaining our roots in the current intellectual milieu while trying to overcome cynicism and detachment is easier said than done. We are calling for nothing less than the re-mythologization of our lives. While not abandoning our outsiders' knowledge of the role of myth and the way it functions, we must be able to take the leap of re-entering the world of myth, in which the constant confrontation with sacred Presence is of the very fabric of daily existence. Our *razo wa-shov* can become a rhythmic rather than a fragmenting process only as we begin to take ourselves seriously as human beings of great spiritual strength. Our weakness of soul is less real than we would sometimes like to believe. Such seriousness and renewed confrontation with our inner strength will come to us as we rediscover who we are, as we claim our place as members (albeit in our own ways) of the eternal faith-community of Israel.

We have always fled because the task is too great, the burden too much to bear. When we heard the Voice say "a kingdom of priests" even before the theophany itself, we knew it was time to run away. Again, in the symbolic person of Jonah, when we saw that it meant transforming *the world*, we turned and fled. Who, us? *The world*? Madness. And so the ghetto, or at least our half of that nefarious bargain. And who is to say that transforming the self is any less a challenge than transforming the world?

Sinai is eternal, its demand infinite, and we want to reject both madness and flight. In learning to live with the rhythm of our inner tides there may be a path that brings some peace. Not the stillness-peace of a lake or a pond: those we strugglers can never attain (and thus we reject them)! Rather the peace of the waters of Ocean, ever churning, smashing, rising, and falling—finding their peace in the regular breathing of tides, seeing themselves and their beauty both in ebb and in flow.

An end to flight?

Who is the man who can stand to live with his own holiness? Perhaps Messiah. Maybe that's what he's all about . . .

NOTES

NOTE: The student of Hasidism will note that much of this article can be taken as a re-reading of Hasidic sources through twentieth-century eyes. The following are some *suggested* points of departure.

1. Benjamin of Zalozhitz, *Ahavat dodim*, Lemberg: 1797, p. 61a. Cf. Rivka Schatz, *Ha-hasidut ke-mistiqa*, p. 117.
2. *Liqute yeqarim*, New York: 1963, p. 6a.
3. *Degel mahaneh Efraim* (*wa-yeze*), Jerusalem: 1963, p. 40.
4. *Hayyim wa-hesed*, Warsaw: 1891, p. 7a.
5. The appropriate Kabbalistic term here is *ha'alat mayyin nuqvin*, the raising up of the "feminine waters," the waters from below which man raises up (as the new manna, one source would have it) to sustain the heavens. On the complicated relationship between *Shabbat* and weekday religious consciousness, cf. *Sefat emet* (*ki tisa*, 1871), v. 2, p. 99a.
6. Seemingly more to be found in such later Polish traditions as those of Izhbitz and Ger.
7. This dominates in early "classical" Hasidism, particularly in the school of Mezritch. Cf. Schatz, *op. cit.* chapter 3 and Hillel Zeitlin, *Be-pardes ha-hasidut weha-qabalah*, chapter 1.
8. Desideratum: A Judaism that allows, even accentuates, its mystical self-understanding, while at the same time radically denying the Hellenistic/Gnostic body-soul and matter-spirit dualisms which have so deeply infected us. Handle carefully and avoid Frankism.

The question of prayer has in the past elicited two equally un-
satisfying approaches in Jewish thought: either dry, scientific
study of the historical development of the text of the prayer-
book, or the unwitting mystification of the experience of prayer
in romantic effusions of theologians. The work of a happy de-
viant, Rav Kook, has yet to be made intelligible to Western
readers.

Alan Mintz, in the following article, attempts to establish
a middle ground by asking what the experience of Jewish
prayer should yield, and how the language of the siddur *(prayer-*
book) might ideally function in this way. The emphasis is
placed not upon radical surgery performed on the text, nor
upon the wholesale inclusion of outside materials into the serv-
ice; hope is placed rather in the possibility of investing the
words of the liturgy with personal and empirical meaning, as
well as the ability to think in ways which are symbolic and
metaphorical rather than confined and literal.

New Metaphors: Jewish Prayer
and Our Situation[*]

by ALAN L. MINTZ

———————

It is a very tenuous assumption that anyone still wants to talk about prayer. Is it on anyone's list of concerns? Does anyone really care? In reality, unless we have to defend prayer to students or non-Jews, we let the subject drop and be swept under the carpet. It has ceased being even problematical. In opposition to this trend, this article makes the claim that although the subject is enormously difficult and the solving of its problems remote, prayer is still worth considering even if our efforts are only "experiments in thought." To initiate critical exploration of prayer by complaining and lambasting would be self-indulgent in addition to echoing what we already know. Discussing prayer has to be a *tabula rasa* affair; we have to disregard

[*] This selection originally appeared in *Response*, Vol. III, No. 1, Spring 1969.

boring formulas, uninviting communal associations and
adolescent prejudices in order to be ready to ask the question "what should prayer be, do, yield?" In order to engage
in useful analysis rather than exhortatory sermonics, we
have to take the onus upon ourselves and project a desired
model. Then might we compare it with the actuality of
Jewish prayer and its expression in the *siddur*.

Among the three tasks we would ascribe to prayer, one
would be *personal integration*. Much has been made of
the fact that technological society tends to divide life into
specialties which are constantly decreasing in scope. For
those of us who are not yet "out in the world," we do not
understand this observation in terms of careers and profes-
sions, but more urgently as regarding the compartmentalization of our lives. Neither the village nor the *shtetl* functions any longer as a totally encompassing institution or as
a community which makes provisions for all our needs and
interests. That kind of cultural totalism is—for better or
for worse—irrevocably lost and has consequently been re-
placed by a swarm of sub-cultures and institutions, each
competing for our involvement and emotional investment.
We depend on college, an activist project, a school of Jewish studies, a summer camp, a synagogue, our roommates
and perhaps the *Response* community each for the fulfillment of different needs. As a natural result of such fragmentation, we play different roles in addressing the members of each community: sharp intellectual, cool activist,
defender of the faith, accessible model to younger kids,
tender lover and so on and so forth. Being not one person
but twenty takes its toll on our inner life, and we quickly
lose any sense of identity, integrity or self.

Our culture and environment have radically altered,
and we have been denied the natural world as a primary
object of wonder. Even though nature has been banished

from the urban imagination, there are other more significant events and relationships in our world through which
we catch glimpses of a more ultimate field of meaning. Indeed, it is the ever-astonishing depths and transformations
of the interpersonal relation which provide a continuously
expanding horizon for the realm of mystery. As relationships both deepen and change, we must go searching continually for the elusive contours of reality. Wonder is the
motivation and prayer the quest. To pray is to re-awaken
to that which is more than the everyday, to become an ex-
plorer into the interconnectedness of things. We reach
upwards in order to come down to a more livable ground
of action.

Recovering lost unities is more than difficult, but
prayer stands the anguished attempt at reintegration, the
painful, groping process of trying to recover one's self.
There is no quick restoration, no easy reconstruction; we
look, instead, for readjusted equilibria and new align-
ments. After trying to identify the nature and variety of
our masks, we struggle to pull these disparate elements
into some new order. We wrestle to hold contradictions in
tension, rediscover priorities and dismiss cheapening in-
volvements. In those wished-for but infrequent moments
when we know "something has happened," we feel the
chaos of competing roles yielding to the realization of pattern and configuration. Prayer as the poetic act of unifying
opposites; the worshiper as poet.

Second, prayer should yield access to the experiencing
of *mystery* and *transcendence*. To explicate these terms is
difficult, but we might think of mystery as recovering a
sense of life as poetry, of everyday happenings as cadences
in a larger, less pedestrian rhythm. Indeed, we can only describe transcendence negatively, that is, in terms of something different in kind than our ordinary arrangements.
Among everyday events there are moments when we discern islands of meaningfulness and pockets of ultimacy

which point beyond themselves. Reality (or divinity, if you will) is then imagined as a network of relationships so complexly and subtly interconnected that we must regard it as ultimately mysterious because we cannot fix and categorize it. Our response becomes a dialectic of wonder: the more we know, the more we are amazed.

Finally, the moral component in prayer is the *awareness of sin*. Despite unwanted Christological associations, sin means falling short of a goal and implies a sense of incompleteness, dissatisfaction and unfulfillment. In our self-assured notions of radical politics and progressive education, we often avert our eyes from our moral insensitivity and capacity for evil. Guilt is the inevitable result of the awareness of wrong-doing. Prayer is not the safety valve which cathartically lessens this anxiety when it becomes too painful, but an apparatus for moral reassessment and recommitment. The worshiper first confronts a list of concerns (in the anthropomorphic system, a catalog of completed symbolic actions performed by God) and, by force of comparison, realizes his own inadequacy in various areas. The other step in the process is the realignment of self, the inevitable recommitment to values that results from a consciousness of sin acquired during the existential assertion of meaning, i.e., prayer. Prayer stands pivotally between relativism and absolutism in offering man a list of concerns to be addressed but without dictating ultimate decisions or personal priorities.

To step back for a few moments, it is not difficult to see that integration, transcendence and sin are categories mysterious unto themselves and repel inroads attempted by discursive language. We certainly possess no knowledge of tools sophisticated and sensitive enough to approach directly such shadowy and elusive provinces. Since we cannot depend on naked, descriptive language (perhaps Kaplan's mistake), we turn instead toward language and its symbolic scaffolding, metaphor. (Non-verbal modes—

drugs and gesture—will be touched on later.) In the thought of Ian T. Ramsey, the religious phrase performs two tasks. First, it renders some aspect of mystery intelligible by picturing it in a model familiar to us (e.g. a clother of the naked), and second, it should evoke and generate within us further personal disclosures into the nature of the cosmos.

This fragile duality of function is presented in a slightly varied way in a saying by Jacob Boehme, the German mystic.

> For according to the outward man, we are in this world, and according to the inward man, we are in the inward world. . . . Since then we are generated out of both worlds, we speak in two languages, and we must be understood also in two languages.

In prayer, the verbal symbol mediates between our inner and outer lives. Metaphor objectifies our inner life and lends structure and pattern to our internal chaos of motives. Our snarled subjective state is temporarily embodied in a symbol so that it can emerge from underground—unsuppressed though structured—into the world of outward expression, if only for a moment. The obverse function of the metaphor is to image, however partially, that outer world, to represent the flux of those shared assumptions about the present and shared hopes for the future we call reality. The best metaphor, then, is one which yields an insight into the world and also lets us plug into it from our personal lives.

But these are very awesome powers we ascribe to the world: to be so pivotal, to evoke so much! Buber's retelling of a Hasidic saying echoes this force.

> You should utter words as though heaven were opened within them and as though you did not put the word into your mouth but as though you entered into the word.

What makes the word capable of sustaining such total investment and engagement? The quality the metaphor must possess is called "empirical fit" (Ramsey). The symbol must reflect our empirical situation, represent the universe that we know in part, refer to our outer and inner realities. It must speak to us, evoke our world of discourse, and let us plug into it. If the empirical fit is not made, the symbol over-extends itself, calcifies and becomes a dysfunctional liturgical fossil.

Discussing the function of religious language provides a natural transition from sketching a paradigm to dealing with the actualities of Jewish prayer as we know it. Our liturgy goes one step further and offers us a full-blown metaphorical system: anthropomorphism. Many models hypothetically could have been chosen, especially the Cartesian one clothed in the garments of the new science, e.g. the inner working of reality represented by sine curves and quantum mechanics. But since we have said that the proper locus of mystery is the interpersonal relation, it is understandable that the system should organize itself around personality as the only model suitably delicate to represent the nuances of the human condition.

The *siddur*, consequently, is the display of the divine personality, the catalog of divine epithets as objects of praise and blessing. God is imagined as the clother of the naked, the sustainer of life, the redeemer, the all merciful, and so on; the composite or summation of all these roles constitutes a super-personality which—as a model—approaches the divine mystery. Once we overcome our pretensions of being able to penetrate directly the eyes of mystery and thus begin to understand the function of anthropomorphism, it need not put us off. If the worshiper can become genuinely engaged in the metaphors, he will realize, at the same moment he affirms the model, which of its aspects he has disregarded in his life action and how he might recreate himself accordingly.

The apparatus is certainly ingenious, but one might well ask whether the particular language of the *siddur* has the power to engage the worshiper to turn him on even if he is so disposed. To better formulate the question: to what extent is this model empirically fitted to what is familiar and urgent to us? Certainly as regards our interest in social activism we cannot complain, viz. the second blessing of the *'amidah:* sustaining life, extending mercy, raising the bowed down, curing the sick, freeing the imprisoned, keeping promises, etc. But when we come in search of reflections of our passion for relationships of sexual love and non-sexual concern and for the dialectic of cultural revolution which so indelibly marks our world, we are disappointed to find only the father-king paradigm. Either the reflections are not there, or they are too obfuscated by impenetrable and sterile language (or perhaps the Protestant understanding of the original which is so much a part of our received Jewish culture). Also the tone of the prayerbook troubles us. We hear an assertion of meaning so unequivocal and self-assured that we find little in common with the tenuous, doubting nature of our existence today. If the liturgical enterprise is to be taken seriously, immediate transfusions of new metaphors are needed, ones sympathetic to our temperament. We might even refurbish and appropriate symbols from the non-rabbinic periods of our culture, e.g. the barely explored riches of Kabbalistic literature. Perhaps we shall yet talk of God as a tender lover or an ever-constant companion.

> *The word as reflection and provocation; so much depends on the word!*

The language that remains has to be re-understood thoroughly, for what we know now as the *siddur* is a disarray of high-church pieties: salvation, redemption, lovingkindness, God as Savior and Deliverer. Only within the scope of utter reinterpretation can we reapproach religious language, a process of re-understanding that would have to be cognizant of cultural revolution and modern temperament. I think we might be surprised to discover radical meanings of the words, in the sense of uncovering their original import and charisma. Some experiments in re-understanding:

hesed (lovingkindness):	endowing another person with a sense of dignity and beauty.
shalom (peace):	minimizing conflict among people by respecting their defense mechanisms.
ge'ulah (redemption):	redemption from depression by a life-restoring event such as falling in love.

In any case, barren literalism is the enemy. In order for the word to function, we must let it hover within a numbus of meaning, different levels of which can be plugged into by the worshiper according to need. After the fashion of Norman O. Brown, we must weaken boundaries of meaning within the word and between the word and our minds. We must be reborn into a symbolic consciousness and inhabit it with courage so that when we utter a word such as *ge'ulah* we may refer to an event at once historical (the Six Day War) and personal (marriage or death).

Even if all these things were done and evocative words really found, we still might wonder whether our consciousness could be made sufficiently non-literal to turn on to words. The revolution we have undergone in technology and communication has had an effect more permeating than any of us would like to admit. We now wander in a brave new world of discursive language where words are either deceitful as in advertising or radically unambiguous as in science. One-dimensionality has set in; symbol reduced to sign. If we do not wish to roll with the tide, two measures commend themselves immediately. On the one hand, we must initiate our minds—or more realistically, those of our children—into the modes of metaphorical thinking: immersion in poetry. On the other, we must put religious poets to work fashioning words which are both genuinely engaging and true to our felt reality.

Will re-educating the religious imagination prove so difficult that we shall have to leave the word in search of other modes of symbolic expression? The answer, of course, is unclear at this time. Any other means would, however, have to fulfill the threefold function we outlined at the beginning. The drug high, as astonishingly documented by Itzik Lodzer (p. 185, this volume) can be used as a vehicle for experiencing transcendence and for responsible religious experimentation. Although it yields quick access to spirituality, we would have to require that such experimentation be related to—perhaps even for the sake of—everyday experience, or "down holiness" as Burt Jacobson calls it. At some point, a moral referent must be present before we can label it *Jewish* prayer. In any case, the rebirth of the senses and the search for the high in many quarters suggests a shared ground of feeling fertile to the growth of prayer.

The techniques of non-verbal communication and self-expression developed at the Esalen Institute and at other laboratory settings in the country hold out other possible new directions for Jewish prayer. The new interest in T-groups with their focus on interpersonal honesty and concern indicate still another path. If prayer is to regain any stature as a community phenomenon, perhaps such groups will be instrumental in providing a communal setting which, for a change, will be a positive factor. Congregational worship and camp services seem inhospitable, and more and more we shall be looking toward small groups of highly motivated religious experimenters who might peel off layers of inhibition and "sing to God a new song."

Often it is precisely the seeming irrelevance of the past to contemporary situations which makes a study of history fruitful; in encountering cultures whose modes of consciousness and experience were radically different from our own, we learn to transcend the "givens" of the present moment by responding to the pull of other realities. How much more exciting is such transcendence when one is studying a past which is in many senses his own! For despite the gaps of time and space which separate the student from his ancestors' text, there is a powerful feeling of personal connection which enables the dialogue to deepen. This is the personal adventure of which we are permitted a glimpse in the following essay.

Michael Fishbane, a member of Havurat Shalom, is a teacher of Bible at Brandeis University. A contributor to the new Encyclopedia Judaica *and to various scholarly journals, he is best known to students in the Boston area for his powerful teaching of texts to the growing number of undergraduates contemplating full-time commitment to Judaic study.*

Lists of graduate students of Judaica and their specific scholarly interests are only beginning to be compiled on a nationwide level, but indications are that the commitment and struggle described in the following piece are representative of an unprecedented number of happy encounters with Jewish study by young American Jews.

Freedom and Belonging:
A Personal Encounter with Judaic Study

by MICHAEL FISHBANE

The story is told of a Moor who, walking wide-eyed down the twisting corridors in the palace of an Oriental potentate, tried to locate himself in the many mirrors along the walls. As mirror reflected mirror, and reflection imaged reflection, space became time and the Moor went mad.

In reflecting upon this deepest of questions, the question of how I came to place Judaic studies at the center of my life, I have often felt such a disorientation; as with the Moor, the confusion lies in trying to locate myself in the mirrors on all sides. When I respond to my appearance in the mirror of a specific issue, I quickly realize that this appearance is but an imaged reflection from other mirrors and other issues. No inexorable logic or dramatic choice among easily separated elements has led me to my present central commitment to Judaic, and especially Biblical studies. Rather, like any real choice and commitment, it is an ongoing one; that is to say, any statement of why I have chosen Jewish texts and historical experience as central to the development of my humanity is really the question of why I *continually* choose it. So in examining my commitment, I search for factors within Jewish text study which both clarify the original choice and, additionally, propel and sustain it in an ongoing resolution.

For me, to engage in Jewish study is to try constantly to bring together two kinds of human experience, two ideal clusters, which are always in tension: the archaic mode of an individual's integration with his cultural past, and the modern mode of his existential freedom. A brief clarification of each mode, the archaic one of integration and the modern one of freedom, is necessary to show just where they impinge on personal life and decision.

The modern, existentialist mode of thought and life develops from its particular notion of time and freedom. In this view, man claims that he "is" only insofar as he makes himself; that time is always and only a fixed present; that man is "shipwrecked," in Ortega y Gasset's language, in a contingent present between a non-existent past and an as yet to be created future. Time is considered discontinuous; the past is viewed as a limitation or constraint upon freedom. This attitude breeds an alienation from one's organic past. Further, this fragmentation experienced on the level of action is also internalized on the level of meaning. In this way one feels isolated in all decisions, condemned by the contingency of all acts, and abandoned to the relativism of all values. Such an alienation in private time is paralleled on the public level. The very illusion that one is not a historically conditioned individual alienates one as a member of culture or community. As a consequence, integration in culture and history is appreciated only as a private, self-conscious act; as a self-proclaimed tragedy of eternal self-overcoming.

Partly in reaction to this predicament, my earliest concern with graduate study was shaped by a desire to locate and study cultures which avoided this alienation by presenting instead an integration of man, culture and history. Interest in the archaic mode of life in non-literate societies was an initial stimulus in this direction. In these societies, such an integration is always realized, because the life and the activities of the gods are eternally reiterated and experienced on the plane of culture. Time presents itself as those cyclical, historical movements in which man re-enacts and shares in the supra-historical life of the gods. Man is intimately involved in the perpetuation of these cycles, for in them lies the truth and possibility of religious and biological life. Just as the actions of the gods established cultural and natural processes, their re-valorization by man perpetuates and sustains them. In such a mode, alienation is a self-alienation from oneself as a responsible creator of the symbols and institutions of his private and public life. True freedom for man lay in living in harmony with and maintaining divine patterns.

I have outlined this mode of archaic integration specifically because my first concern with Biblical studies lay in the desire to experience this phenomenon in the texts of a culture with which I shared a cultural connection. Increased study of these sources brought me into direct contact with the unique mode of integration in the Bible—an integration of man, culture and history through divine covenant and in response to God's will. However, no easy trade-off between the archaic and modern modes occurred. Nor, as I hope to make clear, could the resolution of this tension ever be an accomplished, static fact. Nevertheless, two central and related features were already at work. On the one hand, this early concern for integration was the beginning of my decision to place Jewish sources at a pivotal point in my life. On the other, the immediacy of text study also meant that the life in the text could affect my personal thought and development. The realization deepened that whenever historical materials engage the core of one's life, a personal synthesis is possible. Such a dialogue need never take place at the expense of scholarship and methodological rigor. Rather, it is only after the careful and accurate reconstruction of the materials that a text-dialogue can develop. For in text as in life true meeting takes place only when the integrity of the other is preserved. This idea of immediate text study and the corresponding personal synthesis of the encounter lie at the vital center of why I am and remain in Jewish scholarship, and is my bridge to the wider Jewish community. For in the personal synthesis involved in text-dialogue I have been able to move toward a resolution of the archaic and existential modes of thought. My concern is for a freedom which brings together the personal responsibility of the modern mode with the respect for the structured symbolism of traditional societies. Text study gives the possibility for the freedom of historical consciousness—a consciousness which could integrate and internalize other patterns and experiences, without forfeiting personal responsibility. An elucidation of these statements will be of some significance.

My thoughts take form from the statement by Benedetto Croce, the influential Italian philosopher of history, that "all history is contemporary history." Croce meant, as he says, that history and life have a synthetic function; that history is alive and true to the extent that it is alive and witnessed in the human spirit; otherwise, it is ineffectual and empty. In other words, real history, "the history one really thinks in the act of thinking . . . is the most personal and contemporary of histories." We should certainly say that the matter goes yet further when we move from the task of the historian to his life. To the extent that an area of study also articulates and stimulates important dynamics in the spirit of the historical inquirer which cannot be released when the historical task is completed, this study becomes an ever recurring source of power and self-overcoming. Where historical reconstruction also becomes self-construction, the more ideal freedom of historical consciousness and choice is achieved. The patterns of the Jewish historical past become alive in the receiver, merge with his contemporary complexities, and emerge in a creative synthesis—viable only for him who performs this synthesis in solitude and honesty.

Erik Erikson has often stressed the value of a psychosocial moratorium during identity formation. The value of this hiatus is to provide the integrating ego an opportunity to "try on" new roles and behavior patterns without either the threat of social sanction or the irreversibility of choice. Without overstretching the analogy, I am speaking of a similar, but ongoing attitude toward the Jewish historical past. The concern with a dialogical investigation of Jewish sources is deepened by the concern for developing a new Jewish life-style and language. The structure of this tension demands that ideal freedom which can study and choose from among various types of Jewish living in an attempt to open up a personal path. In this process of listening and response lies the intensely personal and essential nature of midrash, which demands that no synthesis be static, and welcomes the subtle anxiety of each dynamic encounter.

In a daring image the Midrash quotes the biblical verse "This is my God and I will glorify him; my father's God and I will exalt him" (Ex. 15:2) and asks the meaning of this order. In answer, the Masters of Midrash taught that in some historical periods a man who might say "My God" may have trouble in seeing in the events of his time the attributes of a father, the presence of traditional divinity or any reason for praise. What the Midrash teaches on an imagistic level we might paraphrase on the level of historical choice. Thus, Jewish man, he who recognizes and deepens his *humanitas* through contact with Jewish sources, can start from himself alone; he can respond only

wherever commandment is personal. However, in being
open to the meaningfulness of the whole, no part of this
tradition is necessarily excluded from the sphere of direct
revelation, from dialogue and response.

Just as the freedom of historical consciousness stimulates new behavior as it integrates the texts and experiences of various historical articulations, so can the same
freedom provide new options on the level of individual
spirit. By the last I mean that we can appreciate and select
from among various movements of the spirit of great Jewish men, men who have been empowered through the dynamics of a personal Jewish realization. In asking what is
a Jewish man for our time, we must be equally concerned
with how men have been authentically Jewish. Any encounter with the creativity, pain and love of Ibn Gabirol,
for example, transmits freedom through the realization of
how a great spirit synthesized his historical and personal
tensions. Any encounter with Jeremiah cannot fail to confront the reader with the loneliness of spiritual response,
the demand to guard against false gestures, and the command to hear and respond to the voices of the immediate
historical hour.

However, we need not restrict ourselves to the spiritual patterns of "tangible" historical lives, but may turn
also to literary images to clarify and stimulate movements
in our souls. Thus the pericope of Jacob at the Jabbok ford
(Gen. 32:23-32) seizes the reader in its direct power as a
figura in his personal life. I mean this term in both its historical senses. In pagan antiquity the *figura* often meant
"outward appearance" (Varro). Thus I am using it here as
a figurative presentiment of a reality forming in one's soul.
Later it was used by the Church Fathers and Medieval art
with a phenomenal sense. Thus I also am using it as a figurative pointer to a reality as yet unfulfilled. In both these
ways, then, a literary image can be a spiritual coordinate or
foil in one's present contact with past and future. History

overlaps itself when internal and external, personal and communal reality merge. . . .

Who is this Jacob who wrestles with God and man, who is thrown into wrestling with a Nameless One who is also Wondrous? Who struggles for his name, who is Israel even now that he is confirmed as Jacob? Who is this Twisting One, who holds both brother's heel and angel's leg; who dares ask God as angel and God as Man his name, whose asking defines the asker and the asked, for whom answer is not fact but Wonder? Who returns from victory to life even as God, who turns to sing with the morning stars, says: I have wrestled with man and lost—lost the chance to rest, to become an idol fixed Present One (for is not Israel the Eternal Wrestler, the Eternal Questioner?)— but forced to meet man with love as the faced Present One? Who is this Israel who wrestles the God behind the image of the form, who cannot and will not tolerate false gods? Who crosses Jabbok and Jordan and Red Sea and Tigris, who makes God ask: Is this my name? Who struggles from space to time? Who is Jacob? Is he Israel, is he I?

I have been concerned with showing how the freedom of historical consciousness engages and responds to texts on the level of historical articulation, individual integration and figurative imagery. It is important to stress that these three points of contact between text and life may be realized on the communal level. However, since this realization within the wider Jewish community does not take place by itself, but involves the individual movement from the private to the public world, I can best explain its dynamic in terms of my idea of a teacher.

I would stress that every teacher who makes his historical study contemporary with himself is a meeting point of text and life. He authenticates the materials for himself and others by their meeting in his own being. This authentication is even more compelling whenever these texts are placed at the center of his life—so that it is in dialogue with them that he deepens and explores his own humanity.

Each teacher, in this way, by his private response to the materials on the three levels of Jewish historical encounter mentioned before, becomes a fourth level. By embodying a unique synthesis he communicates the freedom of his action and selectivity to his students. He becomes the realization and model of a possibility. However, the student himself must also return to the Jewish sources; he must encounter them himself at his own special point in time. The historical freedom which the student has learned from his teacher becomes the basis for his personal responsibility for integrating and expanding his tradition. A tradition whose bearers are so constituted gives hope for its eternal contemporaneity. Through such a historical freedom new options for growth will be disclosed in each Jewish individual. In the overcoming of notions of an ideal, monolithic Judaism lies the historical freedom in which self-responsible lives can be formed.

Facing the Holocaust

It is revealing that the following poem and story were not written by a poet and short story writer but by graduate students who do not profess much experience with these forms. The point is not to apologize for the writing—it needs no apology—but to imply that in encountering personally the reality of the Holocaust, young Jews seek release from the strictures of discursive thought. Writing essays, theologizing, explaining seem almost beside the point, and on occasion blasphemous.

Barry Holtz wrote his poem as an undergraduate, after hearing Elie Weisel speak at Tufts University. Barry now studies American and religious literature at Brandeis University, and is a member of Havurat Shalom.

Hillel Levine was ordained by the Jewish Theological Seminary (Conservative), received a master's degree in sociology from the New School, and now studies sociology of religion at Harvard and teaches at Havurat Shalom. The story is based upon his experiences in Jerusalem and during a visit to Auschwitz.

For Elie Weisel*

by BARRY W. HOLTZ

Soft coals burning, turning with your head,
Stop, aim at me, flicker, spark, and die—
Passing on.
You walk slowly, stumble into the microphone,
    face the audience
And begin to whisper words
We almost cannot hear.

No one speaks so softly
But wind in flowergardens;
No one speaks so intimately making
Each of us a lover who waits in a dark room,
And like soft coal burning, your eyes are gentle
Touching us lightly, lingering, passing on.

* This poem originally appeared in *Response,* Vol. II, No. 1, Winter 1968.

You say no art can come of suffering
But your face, forged in fire, denies that.
The truth is: You have seen too much—
Men turned to carbon in stone houses is too high
A price for any graven "David" or "Moses."

You say you are only a storyteller
And you spend this night
Softly recalling tales, softly recalling
The poetry that is passing and never written down.
They say when the Temple was in flames,
The Priests threw the keys to the gates
Back to the heavens.
But your eyes, your ancient burning eyes,
Remembering ash and black smoke
Softly curling like a serpent,
Your eyes grasp the keys tightly on earth
With a soft burning light
Eternal and unspeakably gentle.

The Trial

by HILLEL LEVINE

It was three o'clock in the morning, and the city of Jerusalem was asleep. The smell of hot asphalt rose above the market's lingering odors. The silence was disturbed by the occasional cry of a baby or the sigh of an old Jew mourning the destruction of the Temple. The echo of footsteps on cobblestones had an eerie quality. Doors would soon open, busses would grind their gears, hawkers would announce their wares. The world would soon be reborn. Now there was silence.

I made my way through the winding streets of Meah Shearim, into the back entrance of the Russian compound. Nine people were already in line outside the ticket window. Soon someone else appeared out of the dark and joined the line. Then a twelfth and more. Each person stood silent and alone. An archipelago of darkness. Faces contorted, eyes gazing into emptiness. The woman standing behind me looked as though she had once been attractive. Now her eyes were dull, her face was wrinkled. "She is remembering other lines," I thought. "Lines that led to eternity. Perhaps she stood behind him and whispered a reassuring word. Who knows what those eyes have seen . . ." I did not dare to ask her if she remembered the child.

I was a child when I first saw his picture. He might have been my age but the horror he had already seen made him look ancient. His grotesque overcoat fell over his knees. His hands were raised in surrender, perhaps also in prayer. His terrified, bewildered eyes spoke to me of his outrage—a comfortless and unrelenting outrage. I could never think of that child without becoming a child myself.

As the sun rose, people began to shed layers of clothing. Some made themselves more comfortable for the long wait. Occasionally, I would overhear someone tell his neighbor how the announcement that this would be the last day of the trial caught him by surprise. "We'll certainly get in. We're so close to the front," one would say hesitantly. The others would nod with reassurance.

As the hour drew closer to ten o'clock, when the tickets would be distributed, people became anxious and impatient. By now, there were several hundred waiting in the early morning sun. A few men were standing to the side, wrapped in prayer shawls and phylacteries, reciting their morning prayers. There was a good deal of pushing, jostling and shouts of protest when someone was caught trying inconspicuously to break into the line. In different corners, people discussed what they would do if left with Eichmann for an hour. In more serious tones, others were discussing their concentration camp experiences. The woman standing behind me began speaking but not really addressing me. As she talked, I could see her rotting teeth. "He killed my family, my lover, all my reasons for living."

She pointed to the number tattooed on her left arm. "This is what he did to me. But now I will face him, and we will see who has the last laugh!"

At ten o'clock, a policeman appeared in the window and opened it. The line began to push forward. The policeman shouted, "There will be no tickets distributed until this crowd is orderly." People began to move back. "Unfortunately, there are very few places, and most of you will not be able to get into the trial." We who were at the front of the line waited breathlessly as we came closer to the window. At any moment the window might shut, and there would be no more hope of seeing him. The pushing, the tension, the heat made me feel faint. My mind began to wander. The line surged forward and back. . . .

"Auschwitz," the conductor cried in a loud clear voice. It was louder in my mind than the screeching brakes. Auschwitz, a name that I could never forget and never know. I stumbled off the train and walked along the platform, propelled by I did not know what. I was pushed from all sides, a multitude of spirits taking their places in an endless line. I moved with greater uncertainty in each step. At the end of the platform, a tall weed bent in the wind—left, right, left, right. Trembling, I moved closer and closer. Left, right. One way might be to life, the other to death. Yet it hardly seemed to matter at this point. Left, right, left, right. "But I am a child," I wanted to cry out. "What have I done? Why must I suffer because of them?" But the weed has its own rhythm and is not affected by the beat of the heart. The heavens no longer thunder, the earth has been defiled. Even a child has no recourse.

The sign swung over the gate, moving with the rhythm of the weed. Its letters, cut through from side to side, seemed to hang in the air. ARBEIT MACHT FREI. Even the Nazis have a sense of humor. Shouldn't their victims have a good laugh before they die? Who are the jesters now, victims or oppressors? ARBEIT MACHT FREI—work is liberating. The world should know the truth which the Nazis have discovered.

The weed pronounced its judgment. "Son of man," it declared. "Son of man, enter the showers, seek purgation." Head bowed, I followed the well-worn path paved with bones and blood.

He stood in a corner. His arms were still raised, his eyes on fire. Excitedly, I ran to him and embraced him. The walls opened, and we were walking together through Times Square. Our hands were raised, our grotesque coats fell over our knees. We looked up, and the letters of the neon signs rearranged themselves. ARBEIT MACHT FREI. From all directions, backwards, upside down—they flashed the same message. The puffs of smoke from the Camels billboard formed A-R-B-E . . . Cars, buildings, people were bent into the shapes of the letters. A bolt of lightning traced them against a darkening sky.

I was pushed up the two steps before the window. The small stack of tickets was quickly dwindling. Just as I received my ticket, the policeman shouted, "Ladies and gentlemen, much to my regret, there will be no more tickets distributed," and shut the window.

There were cries and protest. The crowd surrounded the building. Some knocked on the windows, others tried to force open the door. The ten of us who had received tickets pushed through in the direction of the courthouse several blocks away. Just as I thought I had escaped the crowd, someone grabbed me from behind and almost knocked me down.

"Give me that ticket."

I turned around. It was the woman who had stood behind me in line tugging at my shirt sleeve.

"Give me that ticket," she said. "You don't deserve it. What do you know of such things? Who did you lose in his gas chambers? You were safe in America while millions of us were being killed."

The sympathy that I felt for this hysterical woman turned into anger and hatred.

"Let go of me," I answered, trying to remain calm. "I have the ticket and I have every right to attend the trial. For me, too, it's important to . . ."

"But you weren't there—you don't know what it was like," she shouted, now half sobbing as we walked along the street.

"No, I was not there," I explained. "But I feel a personal deprivation. My life as a Jew is cut off from the creative sources of Judaism that he and his henchmen destroyed. How can it ever be complete?"

"Personal deprivation," she said. "I will tell you of personal deprivation. He murdered my parents, my brothers and sisters, my lover, everyone dear to me. I must see him and point my finger at him. And you must give me that ticket." She grabbed my arm. Her nails dug into my flesh.

I began again, trying to speak in a convincing tone. "But the fate of all of us is bound up in the . . ."

"What fate?" she screamed. "When they were murdering us did you recognize that fate? When we begged you for visas to escape from hell did you remember that fate? When we watched American bombers flying over the concentration camps and hoped that they would spare a few bombs to slow down the murder, what did you do for us then? It is no new lesson that the world should find a few million Jews dispensible. But how could other Jews have cared so little about us? This I will never understand. What were you and your family doing while they made us into soap? Making money, studying, smothering yourselves in banalities to forget that the world was on fire? Rich American Jew, don't talk to me about fate!"

I ran through the crowd of women with bundles, and porters with carts, pushing everything out of my way. I could listen to her no more and had no strength to fight her off. As I turned into an alley, I could see her running after me about a half a block behind. Her face was flushed, she was waving her hands wildly, and seemed to be screaming something which was drowned out by the late morning traffic. I ran down two alleys and across a court-yard. Trying to catch my breath, I entered a phone booth in front of the courthouse, closed the door, leaned against the wall, and closed my eyes.

"The evidence has been placed before the court," the judge said in deliberate phrases. "Does the prisoner have anything to say in his defense?"

I pressed my face against the wall of the glass booth. Haltingly I said, "But your Honor, I was not there, I was not even born."

"Irrelevant, your Honor," the accuser shouted, leaping to his feet. His voice was familiar, one I had heard many times before. "The prisoner is introducing arguments which are irrelevant to this court." Slowly he moved toward the glass booth and pressed his face against mine on the other side of the glass. I could see myself in his eyes as he said mockingly, "And if you were there, what would you have done?"

The phone booth began to shake. I opened my eyes. Her face was pressed against the glass and she shouted at me to come out . . .

I walked out of the phone booth and found myself be-tween the woman and the guard who was collecting the tickets. Suddenly the woman, with a sardonic grimace, pressed her bare arm against mine. At the sight of the numbers against my skin, I gasped. My hand, extended to give the ticket to the guard, fell into her outstretched hand. I watched her pass through the check points and into the court.

Rabbi Everett Gendler has long been active in civil rights, the peace movement, ecumenism, and most recently as an advocate of a more eclectic and inclusive religious symbology. Rabbi Gendler here reflects an increasing sentiment among young Jews that Judaism has allowed itself to become so historicized that the tie with the natural world has been broken and has ceased to be a source of wonder, energy, and instruction. Another important claim being made in this essay is that established religious groups have beguiled us into thinking that Judaism by its historical nature is a monolithic and normative tradition; any strands or components which are distant from institutional Judaism now, therefore, must be inauthentic and not truly of the tradition. Rabbi Gendler's observations are an articulate dissent and departure from this line of thought.

On the Judaism of Nature

────

by EVERETT GENDLER

Each of us, I think, approaches the official tradition of Judaism with a particular set of inherited tendencies and lived experiences: archetypes, somatotypes, infantile impressions and childhood visions, adolescent agonies and all the rest. For each of us, surely, the living tradition of Judaism must be somehow distinct, different, individual. If not, what is the meaning of our religious being?

I was born in Chariton, Iowa, and lived there eleven years. A small town surrounded by open country, nature was omnipresent. Des Moines, the "city" of my adolescence, also enjoyed her presence. So did I.

Not that I was conscious of it at the time. It seems to me now, in retrospect, that not until after ordination from seminary and a period of time spent in the valley of Mexico did nature as such come more fully to my awareness.

The realization of this awareness took time, its relation to my religious outlook more time still. The entire process, I now know, was furthered by graduate academic studies and by poetry. J. J. Bachofen, Johannes Pedersen, Erich Neumann, Erwin Goodenough, Mircea Eliade, D. H. Lawrence, e. e. cummings, William Blake, Saul Tcherni-chovsky, Lao Tzu, Kenneth Rexroth, the Besht, Reb Nachman: these, finally, were among my latter day teach-ers, and I mention them for others more than for myself. It is true, their names do constitute for me a doxology of sorts, and their effect on me is mildly magical. But perhaps it might be that for a few others as well, with similar sensi-bilities, these men might serve too as the good compan-ions, those who, however indirectly, help make our selves known to ourselves.

From this, then, the re-evaluation of official Judaism, and the pained perception of its present plight: sea-sited synagogues with sea-views bricked over! tree-filled lots with windowless sanctuaries! hill-placed chapels opaque to sunsets! the astonishing indifference to natural sur-roundings!

Was Judaism always this way? I very much doubt it.

However powerful the Biblical assault on ancient na-ture cults, elements of those cults persisted, however puri-fied and sublimated, for centuries thereafter among loyal Jews. This much, I think, is convincingly established by the evidence in Raphael Patai's *The Hebrew Goddess*. This underground stream, flowing from the most ancient of times down to the present, re-emerges strikingly at times—in Kabbalah, Hasidism, and recent Hebrew poets such as Saul Tschernichovsky—as the re-assertion of both the Natural and the Feminine components of religion.

Further, whatever merit there may be to the claim that post-Biblical Judaism is very much an urban develop-ment, it must be remembered that cities until quite re-cently were rarely so totally cut off from natural surroundings as are our present megalopolitan sprawls. However removed from landholding by legal disabilities, the Jews of Eastern Europe were nevertheless constantly aware of it and often envious of those who were privileged to have direct proprietary contact with it. Many are the reminiscences of Hebrew and Yiddish writers which focus on *heder* memories of their natural surroundings. And a perusal of the very moving photos in the Polish Volume *Wooden Synagogues* (by Maria and Kasimierz Piechotka) makes quite vivid the rural locations (at least by our standards) of so many of these incomparably expressive structures.

Important, also, is the evidence from the persistence of various folk customs into recent decades. An especially telling instance concerns *Shavuot,* the least nature-oriented of the three pilgrimage festivals.

> It is a custom to put trees in synagogues and homes on *Shavuot* . . . and to spread grass about in the synagogue . . . to recall that at the giving of the Torah the Jews stood upon a mountain surrounded by foliage. The *Maharil* used to spread fragrant grass and flowers on the floor of the synagogue in celebration of the holiday, and if *Shavuot* fell on Sunday, the *Maharil* would bring them in before *Shabbat* . . . On *Shavuot* the *shamash* used to distribute fragrant grass and herbs to every worshipper in the synagague . . .
>
> —J. D. Eisenstein:
> *A Digest of Jewish Laws and Customs*

And what of the *Seder* traditionally celebrated by the Sephardim on *Tu Bishevat,* when some thirty varieties of fruits, nuts, grains, and wines are consumed with special *kavanot* (intentions) and accompanied by readings from the Bible and the Zohar?

Most significant of all, however, has been the faithfulness of the folk to the rhythms of the moon throughout the ages.

In the biblical period, *Hodesh* or *Rosh Hodesh* (New
Moon) was a holiday at least comparable to the Sabbath.
Commerce was prohibited (Amos 8:5), visits to "men of
God" were customary as on Sabbaths (II Kings 4:23), and
New Moon is grouped with Sabbaths and festivals as a
major holiday in the Jewish religious calendar (Hosea
2:13; II Chron. 2:3, 8:12-13, and others). It is interesting
to note that, quantitatively speaking, the New Moon offer-
ings prescribed in Numbers (28:9-15) and Ezekiel (46:3-
7) exceed those prescribed for Sabbaths.

The moon was, of course, the most visible heavenly
marker of the passage of time. As such, she was essential
to the determination of festivals and sacred celebrations.
At the same time, however, her numinous quality constantly tempted people to worship her (Deut. 17:2-7; Jer.
7:18, 44:15-19). It seems likely, then, that Hayyim
Schauss is correct in suggesting that the prevailing rabbinic attitude toward the moon was also hostile, and that
in so far as *Rosh Hodesh* survived at all, it was due to the
loyalty of the folk, not the representatives of the severely
anti-pagan official tradition (Schauss, *The Jewish Festivals*).

This folk feeling for the moon should not be hard to
comprehend even in our own terms. As Mircea Eliade has
pointed out:

> The sun is always the same, always itself, never in any
> sense "becoming." The moon, on the other hand, is a
> body which waxes, wanes and disappears, a body whose
> existence is subject to the universal law of becoming,
> of birth and death. The moon, like man, has a career
> involving tragedy, for its failing, like man's, ends in
> death. For three nights the starry sky is without a moon.
> But this "death" is followed by a rebirth: the "new
> moon." . . . This perpetual return to its beginning, and
> this ever-recurring cycle make the moon the heavenly
> body above all others concerned with the rhythms of
> life . . . they reveal life repeating itself rhythmically

. . . it might be said that the moon shows man his true human condition; that in a sense man looks at himself, and finds himself anew in the life of the moon.

—*Patterns in Comparative Religion*

Small wonder, then, that a folk desirous of maintaining some significant connection both with cosmic rhythms and with the self should preserve its lunar festivities despite official frowns. Nor is it surprising that women, whose bodily functioning includes built-in, periodic natural rhythms, were most closely related to the lunar rhythms.

Work on Rosh Hodesh is permitted . . . but women are accustomed not to work on Rosh Hodesh . . . weaving and sewing were especially avoided on Rosh Hodesh. . . .

—Eisenstein, *op. cit.*

Other observances on *Rosh Hodesh* include these:

It is a mitzvah (recommended practice) to have an especially ample meal on Rosh Hodesh. . . .
In some countries, Yemen, for example, it is a custom to light candles on the eve of Rosh Hodesh both in the synagogues and on the tables at home, just as on Sabbaths and Festivals. Some people prepare at least one additional special dish in honor of Rosh Hodesh and wear special festive garments.

—Eisenstein, *op. cit.*

Of all this and more, how much is practiced today? Except for the announcement of the new month in the synagogue on the Sabbath preceding—and I do mean new month, not new moon; it is all very calculated, calendrical, and non-lunar—very little, from what I have noticed. As for the ceremony of *kiddush hal'vanah* (the sanctification of the waxing moon), an out-of-door ceremony dating from Talmudic times which requires visual contact with the moon between the third and fifteenth days of the lunar month, and which also includes dancing before the moon

—except for a few Hasidim, how widely is this practiced or even known today? Yet it is prescribed even in the Shulchan Aruch, the classical sixteenth-century code of Jewish law.

These few examples do, I trust, establish that the present Jewish institutional alienation from nature was not always the case, and that it is, in fact, a comparatively recent development.

An attempt to analyze why this has happened would take us far afield and lengthen this essay beyond its appointed limits. More important are some of the psycho-religious consequences of this estrangement from nature.

Two or three poetic formulations are among the best brief statements on this subject that I know.

> Great things are done when Men & Mountains meet;
> This is not done by Jostling in the Street.
>
> —William Blake

> They know not why they love nor wherefore they sicken & die,
> calling that Holy Love which is Envy, Revenge & Cruelty,
> Which separated the stars from the mountains, the mountains from Man
> And left Man, a little grovelling Root outside of Himself.
>
> —William Blake

> Oh, what a catastrophe for man when he cut himself off from the
> rhythm of the year, from his union with the sun and the earth.
> Oh, what a catastrophe, what a maiming of love when it was a
> personal, merely personal feeling, taken away from the rising
> and setting of the sun, and cut off from the magic connection
> of the solstice and the equinox!

That is what is the matter with us.
We are bleeding at the roots, because we are cut off from
  the earth
and sun and stars, and love is a grinning mockery, because,
  poor
blossom, we plucked it from its stem on the tree of Life,
  and
expected it to keep on blooming in our civilized vase on
  the table.

—D. H. Lawrence

Nor should one overlook the important lament by Tcherni-
chovsky over

the distress of a world whose spirit is darkened,
for Tammuz, the beautiful Tammuz is dead.

It seems increasingly clear that whatever the penalties
which man may have suffered when he was subjugated to
nature, his "liberation" from nature has become, in fact,
an alienation which is truly a dreadful freedom. No longer
attuned to the cosmic rhythms about him, increasingly entombed by the contrived, man-made elements of his environment, he neither knows himself as microcosm nor has
any felt, enlivening connection with *chei ha-olamim,* the
Life of the Universe (a term for the Divine which twice
occurs in the traditional morning service).

Where, today, does one find that confirmation of being
expressed in this rabbinic statement?

Whatever the Holy One, blessed be He, created in the
  world, He created in man . . .
He created forests in the world and He created forests in
  man . . .
He created a wind in the world and He created a wind in
  man . . .
A sun in the world and a sun in man . . .
Flowing waters in the world and flowing waters in
  man . . .
Trees in the world and trees in man . . .
Hills in the world and hills in man . . .

Whatever the Holy One, blessed be He, created in His
   world, He created in man.

— *Abot d'Rabi Natan*, Version A, Ch. 31

The self shivers in solitary confinement, and each detached attempt to discern one's true being seems to cata-
pult the self into an abyss, or finds the self facing sets of
mirrors which merely cast further and further back, in diz-
zying regress, that very image of the self which was seeking its substance.

Without grounding in felt being, what of relating, of
love? The ever-shifting, estranged-from-the-universe subjectivity often means simply a mutual sense of being lost
together—hardly a solid basis for a lifelong relationship
which should help children also gain some orientation in
this world.

Also, what does it mean to grow up, as increasing numbers of children do today, with so little contact with other
growing things? How does it affect personal growth when
almost all easily-observed, rapid developmental paradigms are of other-determined end products, not self-
determined growth? What does it mean to have numerous
examples of making and processing all around one, but
few if any examples of that slow, deliberate, self-
determined unfolding of inner potential which is so amazing to watch in the transformation of seed into plant? The
separation from the vegetation cycle may have consequences for the spirit that we have hardly begun to comprehend.

And what may be the effects of this estrangement from
nature on the environmental crisis which we face? It is
hard to imagine that there is no connection between the
devaluation and disregard of nature on the one hand, and
her maltreatment and shameful exploitation on the other.

These considerations, for the most part historical and theoretical, are meant to suggest that a vital and relevant Judaism for this age must begin to reclaim seriously its nature heritage. Such a suggestion has, I think, much to support it as evidenced by the way that people do, in fact, respond to such nature elements. Let me cite a few examples.

For some four summers, we held Friday evening services out of doors at the Jewish Center of Princeton, weather permitting. The setting itself was the attractive lawn behind the sanctuary, flat but ringed by shrubs and bushes, with a number of older, substantial trees in view. The hour of the service was advanced somewhat (from eight fifteen to seven forty-five P.M.) to take full advantage of sunset, twilight, and in late summer, the dusk. Nature elements in the traditional service were emphasized; special readings appropriate to a nature setting were included in the service; periods of silence and meditations on trees and shrubs were part of the worship; and the varying qualities of the "twilights" (*aravim*) were also a focus of attention.

I can report that the reaction to this, among adults as well as young people, was almost universally favorable, and often enthusiastic. In fact, except for a few occasions when the bugs were especially bothersome (no, we did *not* spray!), the out-of-doors services were deeply appreciated by nearly all involved.

Another practice which received a generally favorable response was connected with the morning service of Sabbaths and festivals. When there was no *Bar Mitzvah* and our numbers were not increased by people unfamiliar with the building, on bright days, temperature permitting, we would leave the sanctuary immediately after the *Barchu* and head out of doors. There, under the skies and in the face of the sun, we would chant together that part of the service which celebrates the gift of Light and the radiance of the luminaries. And on days when it was not possible to go out of doors, this part of the service was prefaced by a focusing of attention on the light streaming in through the many windows in the sanctuary. In both cases, the added power of this part of the service was quite perceptible.

Speaking to various groups, I have found that, for the most part, people have responded with considerable interest as nature elements in Judaism were brought to their attention. They often seemed eager to relate to more of these elements in their own lives, and were also extremely appreciative of the nature poetry which I might read on such occasions. Such examples as these could be multiplied if space permitted.

I make no claim that such findings constitute a "scientific" survey of the total scene today. I am convinced, however, that they do represent the expression of a profoundly felt need among many people for a renewed relation to *chei ha-olamim*, the Life of the Universe. I am also convinced that contemporary Judaism, if it is to be a living religion, must respond to this need by a renewed emphasis on those many nature elements which lie dormant, neglected, sublimated, and suppressed within the tradition.

At one period of history it may have been the proper task of Judaism to struggle against nature cults in so far as they represented man's subjugation to nature. Over the centuries, however, the reverse has occurred, reaching a frightening climax in our age: man's almost total alienation from nature. Consequently, one of the crucial religious tasks of our age is to work toward man's integration with nature, with all that implies societally, psychically, and theologically.

The elements of religious renewal are many, and the paths to the Divine various. But for at least some of us in this age the following expresses, far better than we could ourselves, how it appears to us:

> And if you ask me of God, my God,
>   "Where is He that in joy we may worship Him?"
> Here on earth too He lives, not in heaven alone,
>   And this earth He has given to man.
>
> A striking fir, a rich furrow, in them you will find His
>   likeness,
>   His image incarnate in every high mountain.
> Wherever the feeling of life flows—in animals, plants,
>   In stones—there you will find Him embodied.
>
> And His household? All being: the gazelle, the turtle,
>   The shrub, the cloud pregnant with thunder;
> No God disembodied, mere spirit—He is God-In-
>   Creation!
>   That is His name and that is His fame forever!
>
> —Saul Tchernichovsky (c. 1900)
>   (tr. by R. Cover, E. Gendler, and A. Porat)

Epilogue

When we stand back for a moment, these essays taken as a whole must cast a puzzling light. On the one hand, they are so eager to be considered new and fresh, to draw distinctions between themselves and the insights and positions of the established community; yet on the other, the very fabric of discourse is shot through with symbols from the Jewish past, evincing a strong reaching backwards in time, an impulse toward re-authentication. But is this not the incongruence we find in any of the movements of creativity in Jewish history, when a generation confronts Judaism with unserviced needs? We find ourselves, our empirical reality, the pressures of the current sense of crisis, on one side; Judaism both as a reservoir of symbols and experiences and as an Other making religious and ethical demands on us, on the other side. Such are the terms of the dialectic we are engaged in, refusing either to become receptacles of the past or one-dimensional cut-outs of the present. And the dialectic is not to be romanticized; it is as trying and anxious as any encounter between self and other in which both parties admit the possibility of being changed.

Within Jewish history, the pendulum which swings between renewal and sterility moves erratically. If the "new Jews" are to make the future yield working models of their vision, they will have to ask themselves a great many serious questions. The communal experimenters, for example, will have to ask themselves whether they have made only post-adolescent stops along the way to the outer world, or whether their communes can remain workable while their members have families and have to make a living. Will the *havurot* resist a tendency to be largely inner-directed? Will they wish to impinge upon the larger community through political means? And perhaps the greater question: Does the small, organic community as a form have applicability beyond the pale of the counter-culture?

Political radicals will also have to make decisions. How will they see their relationship to the Jewish community? If Judaism is mainly the bond which facilitates community organizing and ethnic self-consciousness, to what extent is it being unfairly exploited? Will those few young Jews who make the internal restructuring of the Jewish community their goal be able to withstand the labyrinthian, interlocking bureaucracies they will find?

In their search for a sympathetic past will young Jews seek out and celebrate new aspects of the tradition and now-ignored moments in Jewish history? Will they produce new observances and practices which will make their way into the flow of American Jewish life? Will they evolve new ways of studying Judaism, ones which do not necessarily depend on charismatic figures for their excitement? And finally, will there ever be a convergence between the pressure for ethical and concrete action (as in the Arzt essay) and the mystical journey (as in the Lodzer and Green essays) into an integrated philosophy? These indeed are the considerations which will indicate whether the phenomenon described in the book is of ephemeral or enduring significance.

It is of course true that Jewish radicalism is fueled by much of the same anger and critique that powers general American radicalism. It would be fair, however, to indicate several favorable differences which might enable us to talk in terms of a contribution on the part of young Jews to the American radical community. The tone and substance of this book might suggest indirectly some of the shortcomings of the latter, along the following lines.

It is important for the radical to have a deep awareness of his location in history and a sensitive knowledge of the past as composed both of moments with which he can resonate and others he must reject. This rootedness in history contrasts sharply with much radical consciousness which perceives the act of negation and critique as a moment isolated in time with no perspective forward or backward. Such ahistoricism ends in false messianism and a refusal to accept responsibility from the past and for the future.

The possibilities of particularism recommend themselves also. For some time now we have liberated ourselves from the progressive, reasoned, uniform image of man in which all enlightened universalists partake. We have learned that a rich sense of identity means expression through unique symbols and differing customs. By eliminating our cultural backgrounds, we seem to limit the modes of authentic being available to us. This price is too high to pay for membership in any community of the "arrived," radical or otherwise.

The capacity for spiritual experience is a particularly valuable and healthful possession, one much sought after by many of the contributors to this volume. To be able to disengage oneself from process and gain perspective on one's involvement in the world, to be able to eat with others in a spirit of holiness and reverence, to be able to celebrate life moments with worship and festivity—all these capacities must be essential to the make-up of he who wishes to work in the world for peace and liberation. We need not dwell on the humanizing effect of life-in-community so stressed in this book.

And finally, we point to affirmation as the quality by which young Jews might want to be known to their American contemporaries. Not in the inevitable anguish of opposition, but in the everyday struggle to realize the divine vision, do they discover and unfold themselves. In that sense, each essay here is an experiment in thought, a tentative pause and assessment to prepare the ground for action that is historically grounded, culturally viable, and spiritually engaging.

A.M.

About the Editors

JAMES A. SLEEPER, *a native of Springfield, Massachusetts, received his A.B. from Yale in 1969. With Alan Mintz, he was a founder and editor of* Response *magazine. Mr. Sleeper is currently working toward his doctorate at the Harvard Graduate School of Education.*

ALAN L. MINTZ *was born in Worcester, Massachusetts. He attended Columbia College. He was co-founder and managing editor of* Response, *and was instrumental in creating the New York Havurah, of which he is a member. A doctoral student at Columbia, he is now studying English literature.*